If you want to make a difference with the resources you have, invite Raymond Harris to share his experience on how to be an effective steward. Reading *Enduring Wealth* will change the way you invest in God's work in this world.

Stan Jantz, best-selling author; CEO, Come and See Foundation

As a Christian who participated in the world of business for over forty years, I always struggled with the integration of my wealth and faith. I greatly admire how Raymond has thoughtfully developed an understanding of wealth from a biblical perspective and has invested his wealth in the kingdom in an intentional way that increases human flourishing. My goal is to integrate many of his beliefs and principles described in these pages into my ministry going forward. This is a must-read for anyone questioning the purpose of work and use of their wealth accumulation.

David Ridley, founder and CEO, Invesco Real Estate; guest speaker;
mentor

Raymond Harris is the real deal! Read this book, and you will witness a man devoted to stewardship. My friend Raymond wrote *Enduring Wealth* based on both Scripture and a life of experience (with ups and downs and lessons learned) as he has attempted to be effective and efficient in how he uses the resources God has given him for His glory.

Bob Doll, chief investment officer, Crossmark Global Investments;
former chief equity strategist or investment officer, Nuveen, BlackRock,
Merrill (formerly Merrill Lynch), and OppenheimerFunds

Many men and women create wealth, but few understand its purpose. This book is a treasure map, the shortcut for us to learn what took Raymond Harris years to uncover. As a highly successful architect, Raymond has thought deeply about God's designs for wealth, but even more importantly, he has learned to live them out. I'm proud to call Raymond Harris a friend and an exemplary gospel patron.

John Rinehart, founder and CEO, Gospel Patrons; author, *Gospel Patrons*

Raymond Harris has the courage to write this needed and excellent book. It contains authentic stories that may challenge your way of thinking about generosity. He shares how to convert earthly assets into kingdom capital that you will be able to enjoy for all eternity.

Howard Dayton, founder, Crown Financial Ministries and Compass— Finances God's Way; author

I'm a richer man after reading this book. I love the way that Raymond has tackled a topic that is on the minds and hearts of all of us. I wholeheartedly recommend this book for every faith-driven entrepreneur and faith-driven investor.

Henry Kaestner, cofounder, Faith Driven Entrepreneur and Faith Driven Investor; cofounder, Sovereign's Capital, Bandwidth, and Republic Wireless

My friend Raymond is as kingdom minded and gospel focused as anyone I know in the business world. He and his family want their lives to count for the few things that will last forever and matter most. This focus drives his and his wife's every decision. They live within the reality of "to whom much is given much is required," and this helps them make the most of every opportunity. Their stewardship is bearing enduring fruit, and I have no doubt they will hear our Lord say, "Well done." God gave them many talents, and they are investing them wisely and offering all the return back to God. You'll enjoy Raymond's story in *Enduring Wealth*.

Todd Peterson, NFL placekicker (1993–2005); chairman, Pro Athletes Outreach; former CEO, Seed Company; founder, illumiNations

Raymond presents a new and dynamic perspective on giving and stewardship. His creative use of stories powerfully captures this radical way to invest in God's kingdom. The resulting approach will change your view of donating and, in the process, put you in a better position to convert your earthly assets into real kingdom capital that will endure through eternity.

Thomas C. Leppert, business executive; former CEO, Turner Corporation; former mayor, Dallas, Texas

I've been waiting for this book for five years—ever since the day Raymond Harris told me he was trying to figure out how one converts the currency of the world into the treasures of heaven (see Matthew 6:20). His answer is a stunning vision of God's kingdom economy. This extraordinarily personal and practical book will prove valuable for anyone, but it's especially relevant for the rich and those who partner with them. It should be a required textbook for the growing impact and faith-driven investment communities and every Christian nonprofit. I am deeply blessed to know Raymond as a friend, and reading his book is like having a conversation with him. He's simply the real deal.

Bill Hendricks, president, The Giftedness Center; executive director of Christian Leadership, The Hendricks Center at Dallas Theological Seminary

Enduring Wealth provides valuable insights into the beliefs and practices that guide this committed business leader, husband, father, investor, donor, and faithful steward. Raymond writes with both candor and care for those who yearn for a more meaningful relationship with Jesus and money.

Chuck Bentley, CEO, Crown Financial Ministries; founder, Christian Economic Forum; author

Conversations about money cause some to feel guilty and others to feel weary, but this book by Raymond Harris will leave you feeling inspired and empowered. Substantiated by personal examples, *Enduring Wealth* provides a refreshing and godly take on how to think about money. With grace and conviction, Raymond shares how you can experience the joy that comes from powering God's economic engine for the glory of His name.

Nick Pitts, PhD, former executive director, Institute of Global Engagement at Dallas Baptist University; current events blogger

I learned years ago from one of my ministry mentors the value of being a student of great people—people great in character and godly wisdom. Therefore, you need this book by my friend Raymond Harris. God has blessed all of us with resources. Be a student and learn from the best. Raymond doesn't just talk it. He walks it.

Mark M. Yarbrough, president, Dallas Theological Seminary

The title and subtitle for Raymond Harris's masterful book are perfect descriptions of the challenge he puts before us. What does it mean to be "rich in this world and the next"? How do you build "enduring wealth"? The candor with which he shares his personal stories—successes and failures—provides insight for reflection. If you want to be on the path to hearing God say, "Well done, good and faithful servant," and building enduring wealth, I recommend you read Raymond's book with a pen in hand.

David Simms, managing partner and founder, Talanton; former president, Opportunity US; former White House Fellow

Raymond Harris draws on his wealth of experience in effectively earning, managing, sharing, and investing the substantial material resources God has entrusted to him. Regardless of the magnitude of their financial portfolio, *Enduring Wealth* is a crucial read for anyone who aspires to hear their Master say, "Well done." For those with significant financial assets, Harris shows a pathway to unlocking untapped kingdom potential and envision possibilities you may not have considered before.

William C. Peel, DMin, president and founder, 24Seven Project (24SevenFaith.com); author

Enduring Wealth is a compelling reflection on a lifetime of stewarding God's resources to build God's kingdom. Raymond's experiences and insights are worth reading for anyone interested in how to be increasingly rich toward God.

Todd Harper, cofounder, Generous Giving

I have loved reading Raymond Harris's book. Not only does it help us think with honesty and excitement about the money and gifts God has given us, but it also comes from Raymond, one person who ruthlessly practices these principles. He is a true partner who prays, encourages, advises, and pours himself wholeheartedly into people and projects of eternal worth.

Keith Getty, modern hymn writer and Grammy-nominated artist, Getty Music

Raymond Harris has creatively invested his life and his finances in God's kingdom for decades. When he speaks—or writes—I listen.

Alan Barnhart, CEO, Barnhart Crane & Rigging

Raymond Harris has done it again. This is a must-read book for kingdom leaders. This powerfully insightful book with practical wisdom is sure to make an eternal impact.

Adam C. Wright, PhD, president, Dallas Baptist University

Enduring Wealth is more than just a book on stewardship. It is an autobiographical compilation of a lifelong spiritual journey that the Lord has taken Raymond Harris on. I have been blessed to be a recipient of Raymond's stewardship, and I have learned countless lessons from his perspective on stewarding God's resources. I believe anyone who reads this work will be challenged and inspired to look at their own resources through a new lens and will learn how they, too, have been entrusted to make an impact for eternity.

Nathan H. Sheets, CEO, Nature Nate's Honey Company

In this deeply personal book, Raymond Harris shares a lifetime of lessons of how to steward the money entrusted to us. He shows us how we can loosen our grasp, open our hands, adopt an eternal perspective, and then invest wisely and well in what will last.

Mark Holman, CEO and chairman, Expanesthetics Inc.

ENDURING
WEALTH

Being Rich
in This World
and the Next

RAYMOND HARRIS

BroadStreet
PUBLISHING

BroadStreet Publishing® Group, LLC

Savage, Minnesota, USA

BroadStreetPublishing.com

Enduring Wealth: Being Rich in This World and the Next

Copyright © 2024 Raymond Harris

9781424568826 (hardcover)

9781424568833 (ebook)

Cover and interior by Garborg Design Works | garborgdesign.com

Printed in China

24 25 26 27 28 5 4 3 2 1

CONTENTS

Chapter 1

REDEFINING WEALTH

MEETING JOHN ENRIGHT

After a brutal twenty-hour flight, we arrived in Cape Town, South Africa. I was traveling with a group of businessmen looking for opportunities to invest in African businesses that would help Christian ministries become sustainable. Our entourage toured several places before getting to Lusaka, Zambia. From there we took a long van ride on a two-lane road to Ndola in northern Zambia, just short of Congo.

I was warned, "You will be meeting with a pastor named John Enright. He has quite a different viewpoint from what you probably expect. Watch out."

Upon arrival at John's Kafakumba pastor-training school, we were greeted with a warm smile and cold iced tea. Quite a treat for weary travelers in the African summer.

Sitting on a green concrete patio on the front porch of John's home, I saw a lot of activity. But I heard even more: a sawmill in the background along with the distant chattering of workers. Over my left shoulder was the school and the sound of a class in session.

John began to tell a little bit about his story and how Kafakumba began, saying, "I grew up in a mud hut, the son of missionary parents in Congo." He now knew five languages fluently, was immersed in the culture, and, although part American, was "all African." John waved his hands as he talked about God's kingdom and how important it was to work effectively in it. "I decided long ago that business was one of the best ways to spread the gospel," he said. "It has enabled me to support myself as well as the numerous pastors who come to be trained in the center."

I studied John's eyes and saw something I've seldom seen before—and had been warned about. He was not wild-eyed, but you could see a spirit of godliness and eternal vision in his gaze. Some would classify him as bombastic, but I saw a resemblance to the personality of my own father.

John continued, "I want businesses to support my ministry work so I don't have to rely on US donations. And I'll tell you frankly, many American missionaries here are painfully ineffective."

Obviously opinionated, he seemed to know what he believed. And he lived it out. Some of the guys in our group were taken aback by what he was saying, but I was drawn in. As I listened intently, I began to feel the Holy Spirit over my shoulder saying, *I want you to be involved with John.* This quiet whisper in the back of my mind made me listen even more intently.

On the trip back to Cape Town, from where we would fly back to America, I wondered what my involvement might be. I didn't know this man, but I was intrigued by what he had said. And I certainly agreed with the idea of sustainable missions. But what could I do? The Holy Spirit seemed to say, *I want you to invest $250,000 in John's businesses.*

Back home, I talked to my wife, Marydel. She was support-ive, and we sent the money through another mission organiza-tion. I took this step to remain anonymous. Not yet knowing John well, I didn't want to adversely influence an undeveloped relationship by causing John to see me only as a "money man" for whatever he needed.

The mission organization I had chosen to distribute the money wanted to divide it so that a portion could go to another project in a neighboring country. Because I didn't know John well yet—but I did have confidence in this organization—I acquiesced. The plan was not exactly what I had heard the Holy Spirit tell me, but the logic seemed reasonable. John received $100,000 while the other effort received $150,000. Although a bit confused, I trusted this other organization's wisdom.

What I did not know was that John truly needed the money. It may seem weird that a missionary would be in this much financial trouble, but his circumstances were unusual. The unstable Zambian economy forced him to borrow money at exorbitant interest rates from the local bank. He needed capital to build the economic engine that would keep his work running sustainably and avoid future debt. I'll talk more about economic engines later, but suffice it to say that John was truly building a business model that would support not only his ministry but also thousands of Zambian villagers.

I developed a long-distance friendship with John over the next year. I soon returned to Zambia after the Holy Spirit prompted me again to help John with his ministry. Traveling with several Christian friends, we arrived at John's house in Ndola, and he greeted us warmly. Then John took just three of us to a back room of his house.

Looking directly at me, John said, "You're the one who sent the money earlier."

"Yes," I said. "How did you know?"

"I just figured it out."

"Well, let me tell you what I've figured out," I said. "I believe that the Holy Spirit had led me to give you a larger amount at the outset. I agreed to an adjustment of that plan, but I am convinced that the original amount I was prompted to give is still the right amount. So I've come with another $150,000."

John began to cry. And, of course, I joined him. I can't explain it; I was just overwhelmed with emotion. The whole room was.

"You don't know what this means," John said. "I was into the bank for $150,000 at a 30 percent interest rate, and I just couldn't make the payments. The money you are bringing is the exact amount needed to cancel the debt. This will make our ministry and our businesses whole."

He paused to steady his emotions. "And another thing. A man in my church came to me awhile back. He prophesied that a man would be coming to bring exactly the money we needed and that he would be coming with a group of fellows. You see, this prophecy given to me several months ago has now been fulfilled in this room."

I was floored by what God was doing behind the scenes. The Holy Spirit seemed to be orchestrating not only the first gift but also the timing of the second gift in order to build a relationship with John. Although the first gift was originally anonymous, the second gift was given with full disclosure as a blessing.

This began a wonderful relationship over the next ten years. Together John and I developed a flourishing business model. There were many failures. In fact, we experienced nine business failures before the two major businesses worked. But the ones that worked *really* worked—on a scale that's hard to imagine.

Now you know how this story of unusual stewardship began. I'll tell you more of my journey with John later.

ARE YOU RICH?

While traveling frequently around the world, I've noticed the poverty and pain that plague the masses. Walking among the poor on five continents over the past ten years has brought me face-to-face with an unshakable reality: much of the world barely survives from day to day. The ravages of poverty create problems so complex that they seem unsolvable. In fact, I believe that poverty is one of the most complicated problems on earth.

You will probably say that you are not rich because you know many people who have more than you. But compared to most of the world's population, I bet that your financial net worth makes you very rich. I have been blessed to live in comfort, wealth, and privilege far beyond most of the world. I realize that this is a gift from God and not just the product of my own doing. First Chronicles 29:12 states, "Both riches and honor come from you, and you rule over all. In your hand are power and might, and in your hand it is to make great and to give strength to all."

The world assumes that the value of life is measured by possessions, but Jesus, in Luke 12:15, warns us to be on guard against that false assumption. We don't work just to accumulate, spend, or save. It's about more than just our needs and those of our family. The obsession to make as much money as possible and accumulate as much as possible in this life is shortsighted. Making money and accumulating wealth can be a great blessing. But if we miss the main purpose, we end up with possessions that disappoint us in this life and will not accompany us in death.

When Jesus talked about the financially wealthy on earth, it was usually in contrast to the poor on earth who had wealth in heaven. He never condemned the rich for being rich but for trusting in their riches and remaining blind to God's purposes because of their riches. To them, He issued serious warnings, all the while demonstrating that true wealth has ultimate and eternal importance and is stored and transported in the heart.

The real question is this: Are you rich in God's economy? As rich as the poor widow who gave her last coin? Jesus knew her heart, her love, and her trust, and that was worth a fortune to Him. This is the wealth we should seek.

ACCOUNTABILITY AHEAD

I also know that God will hold me accountable for this wealth and privilege. He will ask how I used my status, position, comfort—all my resources. He will ask me if I used them for His kingdom purposes or if I buried them on earth like the lazy servant in the parable of the talents (Matthew 25:14–30). Have I ever demonstrated a willingness to suffer to ensure the proper distribution of wealth to others? Was I willing to work hard to ensure that others had the benefit of what they needed? Did I see my wealth as a divine opportunity to be the hands and feet of Christ? Or did I count it all as my own to squander?

Nothing shakes me to the core like the thought of standing before Jesus and recounting how I used what He entrusted to me. This should keep stewards awake at night.

GOD'S DESIGN FOR OUR WEALTH

Why do we then strive to accumulate wealth and possessions? We must realize that wealth is a gift from God, who owns and controls the earth and everything in it. "Yours, O LORD, is the greatness and the power and the glory and the victory and the majesty, for all that is in the heavens and in the earth is yours" (1 Chronicles 29:11). Without this realization, wealth and possessions will never fulfill us. The same old materialism will never satisfy the deep longing of our heart. Isn't it odd that most men and women desire wealth but few know its true purpose and the joy of using it properly? When striving for mere riches, even when they succeed, they fail to find contentment.

It makes me ask what God's design for our wealth is. Only God can give us the ability to enjoy our wealth. His design is that we are to serve His kingdom with the wealth entrusted to us. Every man and woman should be on a journey to determine how they are to fulfill God's design in their own life. I have found that you cannot tell someone how to spend money. Everyone must come to grips with why God endowed them with wealth. Only then can the struggle to find contentment have a good ending: God gives it as part of His design.

WEALTH IS MORE THAN JUST MONEY

A wealthy person in God's kingdom is defined by much more than their financial balance sheet. Money is only one form of wealth. A truly wealthy person, if stripped of their money, may well become wealthy again by their giftedness to generate more.

As a young boy, I remember hearing of some Jewish businessmen who had their physical assets confiscated during World War II. They became wealthy again because they retained the talent and wealth-building habits that had generated their original assets. If you move someone with these abilities to any new place, their family will be wealthy by the next generation. It's a generalization to be sure, but the principle stands: you may strip the physical assets from a wealthy person, but if they generated them to begin with, they are likely to regenerate future wealth.

DEFINING WEALTH

The same is true in God's kingdom. Wealth might be measured by accumulated assets, but those assets involve much more than commodities, real estate, cash, or collectibles. The most important asset is the set of characteristics and commitments within a person—the ability to continue generating assets for the eternal kingdom.

I think we can also define *wealth* as successfully using the giftedness God has given to each person. This type of wealth includes the ability to influence people through leadership, the ability to convene and collaborate for the building up of God's people. It also includes artistic and intellectual abilities used to bring joy and beauty in God's creation. Far more than mere financial assets, wealth is the use of our essence to build God's kingdom on this earth.

PURPOSES FOR ACCUMULATING WEALTH

What is my purpose for accumulating financial wealth? I have often contemplated the question. Is the accumulation of wealth and assets part of our human nature and worldliness, or is this God's plan for us? Many Christians equate wealth with something less than holy. Although the love of money is a source of sin, money itself is neutral, and we can use it for great benefit. Anything used for the glory of God becomes holy in that use. If God grants wealth to certain people, His intention is for them to use it to glorify Him.

Accumulated wealth of all kinds can help us for eternity if we realize our purpose is to be a conduit of God's love and provision. There is everything holy in making significant money if we understand the purpose behind it. But if we stockpile or hoard it because of fear of not having enough, it fails God's intended design for it.

Let's look at purposes for accumulating financial wealth:

1. For leisure and pleasure
2. For security
3. For an improved lifestyle
4. For investments
5. For posterity and inheritance
6. To take care of family

7. To take care of others
8. To expand God's kingdom

God will hold all people accountable for their accumulated wealth. We know that "everyone to whom much was given, of him much will be required" (Luke 12:48). We also know that our wealth will testify against us in the final judgment as we stand before God (James 5:3). With this accountability in mind, I think it wise for the rich man or woman to use their wealth in a manner that glorifies God in accordance with His purposes.

LEISURE AND PLEASURE

I love to go on vacation. There are things in life that give pleasure, and that is good. If, however, life consists of mostly leisure and pleasure, then this use of wealth is self-serving, especially while others suffer from want.

SECURITY

There is certainly nothing wrong with using financial wealth to help us become secure. If we, however, trust in our wealth for our security, we have created an idol to replace God's role as our provider. Wise people prepare for the future to take care of themselves and their families so they won't be a burden to others. Financial security is not a bad thing as long as we don't make it the main thing or place our confidence in our accounts rather than in God. He is the one who provided them and sustains them. God owns us and everything we have.

LIFESTYLE

Should we use our financial wealth to improve our lifestyle? Sometimes yes, sometimes no. It would be difficult to effectively help others if you lived in abject poverty. Motivation and balance come into play. Is your heart focused more on living a life of leisure or being effective for God's kingdom? Improving your lifestyle is certainly not bad, but it should be balanced with the realization that most people around the world do not have basic necessities. How far are you willing to indulge yourself while others do without? No one can answer these questions for you; God designs and deals with each of us uniquely.

INVESTMENTS

How about investments? You can't make them if you don't have money. You must accumulate to be able to invest and provide for the future. Financial margin is the ability to invest when opportunities arise. We never know when something will come along that will be good for investment. But again we must look to the purpose of investing: if it is solely to make more money, it is an unholy end in itself. But if there is a greater purpose—one in keeping with God's design—it becomes a holy endeavor.

SUCCEEDING GENERATIONS

Do we leave our money to posterity or children? It is generally good to leave an inheritance to your children and to your grandchildren as a blessing. I will share two cautions. First, don't harm them unintentionally by giving them more than they can handle without limiting their self-development, responsibility, and work ethic. Otherwise the blessing of wealth can quickly become a curse.

Second, don't relegate your stewardship responsibility to future generations. One of your most important responsibilities is to develop and model what it means to walk with Christ and the values of a good steward. It's good to tell them about giving. It's far better to model it and to find ways to do it *with* them.

How do you answer this question: Which is the greater privilege for your children—to have your money to live on or to have training opportunities for them to become stewards? I've noticed that money very seldom passes through to the third generation of a family. The second generation usually consumes it, eliminating it by the third and often leaving a bitter trail of dysfunction and destruction. There are few instances where financial wealth transfers down through the generations, successfully satisfying God's design for it.

FAMILY

It is our responsibility to take care of our family in a manner appropriate for them. The apostle Paul encouraged the early church to look to the needs of the family by writing, "If anyone does not provide for his relatives, and especially for member of his household, he has denied the faith and is worse than an unbeliever" (1 Timothy 5:8).

OTHERS

We are to look to the needs of others just as ourselves. That is the essence of the second great commandment. About this, the apostle Paul wrote, "Let each of you look not only to his own interests, but also to the interests of others" (Philippians 2:4).

KINGDOM PURPOSES

Using accumulated wealth for God's kingdom is a tricky subject. Is giving money an investment in God's kingdom? Sometimes yes, sometimes no; it depends on who the recipient is and how they steward that money into the kingdom. Sometimes starting or supporting businesses that help others may yield a better return than giving to a nonprofit or a ministry.

Marydel and I have invested in a honey business in Africa that generates nine thousand jobs and gives earned income to the poorest of the poor, bringing them out of debilitating poverty. We've also used investments in a for-profit business to help women escape sexual slavery and abuse by providing employment, housing, and protection. We have invested in projects that provide health care in some of the poorest countries in central Africa. Some projects generate sufficient income to be self-sustaining; others provide necessary medical care but require continual funding.

Taking care of the poor is a great use of accumulated wealth. Although few metrics exist to document the return on this kind of investment, God knows and keeps an accounting for us. Taking care of the poor is on His heart. After all, the poor will be the rich in faith in His upside-down economy. Simply feeding people and clothing them is not a waste. It is an honorable use of accumulated wealth that also helps restore dignity stolen by life circumstances.

God gives us wealth in all its forms so we can work in His kingdom's economy to serve our stewardship purpose in life. We know that God gives wisdom. If we don't have it, he will give it to us if we ask. "If any of you lacks wisdom, let him ask God, who gives generously to all without reproach, and it will be given him" (James 1:5). And we saw earlier that He gives financial wealth. He entrusts both to our stewardship.

AVOIDING THE BAD RAP

It is obvious that not all rich people steward what God has entrusted to them for His intended purposes. Most have a bad rap because of the perception that they spend it on themselves or leave it to future generations in lieu of taking care of God's kingdom while they have the opportunity. Fortunately, there seems to be a growing number of exceptions—wealthy individuals who are becoming wise (and blessed) stewards.

Since God is the grantor of wisdom and wealth, we must understand His purposes if we hope to have success as stewards in His economy. We become God's hands and feet as we use wealth for righteous purposes to make the whole society flourish.

The question is what a rich person should do with their resources. The first chapter of Isaiah gives us an extensive picture of God's displeasure with our rituals and even our offerings to Him if they are unaccompanied by doing right. Isaiah 1:17 says, "Learn to do right; seek justice. Defend the oppressed. Take up the cause of the fatherless; plead the case of the widow" (NIV). Paul, in 2 Corinthians 9:10–11, sheds further light on God's strategy for enriching His stewards: "He who supplies seed to the sower and bread for food will supply and multiply your seed for sowing and increase the harvest of your righteousness. You will be enriched in every way to be generous in every way, which through us will produce thanksgiving to God." God blesses His stewards so that they can be a blessing to others.

Here's a follow-up question: Who among us is wise for eternity? Those who use their accumulated wealth to honor the Lord in obedience to His direction for the wealth He has entrusted.

LIFESTYLE REVELATION

Because of our human nature, our hearts are tied to this earth and our money. If we can separate our heart—even for a moment—from our money and possessions, we will see God's kingdom and eternity more clearly. Nothing obscures the view of eternity more than earthly treasures and distracting possessions.

If we truly believe that we are earthly sojourners awaiting our permanent home in heaven, it will show in how we handle our money. What we treat as important reveals the true love and focus of our heart. If our home is in eternity with Christ, then our focused efforts and resources will promote Christ and His kingdom. Our lifestyle reveals what we value most.

Chapter 2

IT'S OKAY TO BE RICH

JESUS IS THE RICHEST OF ALL

Jesus is the richest of all time and will be forevermore. Just think about the wealth in the hands of Christ, who owns everything. What Jesus chose to do with His wealth sets the standard. He is our example of how to be a rich man or woman in God's economy and kingdom. Paul described what Jesus did in 2 Corinthians 8:9, "You know the grace of our Lord Jesus Christ, that though he was rich, yet for your sake he became poor, so that you by his poverty might become rich."

Jesus left the wealthiest neighborhood in the universe to reside with us. Although rich, He gave up rights to His wealth and became poor so that we might eventually become rich through our inheritance as God's sons and daughters. He promises to take those who love Him back home to His neighborhood so we, too, might live with Him for eternity in mansions connected with streets of gold.

Jesus entered the world as a poor man. The Holy Spirit conceived the Son of God to a poor teenager betrothed to her future husband. Born in a barn and placed in an animal feeding trough in the humblest of circumstances, He grew up in a poor community undistinguished by anything of notable value. One of the disciples asked regarding Jesus, "Can anything good come out of Nazareth?" (John 1:46). Jesus grew up without much money, although He worked hard with His earthly father as a carpenter.

Living much of His adult life as a homeless man, Jesus was totally dependent on the provision of others during His last three years. During His last week, He rode into the city of Jerusalem on a borrowed donkey and used a borrowed room to celebrate a final supper with friends. Soldiers took Jesus' garments from Him in front of others while He hung on a cross. Onlookers ridiculed Him as He died a humiliating death, a victim of injustice. Later that day, Jesus was buried in a tomb not his own, owned by a wealthy man.

All this was by divine choice so He could relate to the abused, the homeless, the poor, the single mothers, the unmarried who choose to keep their children, and the children conceived out of wedlock. Jesus chose to become poor, to live among the poor, to understand their plight so they might have eternal life and become rich in eternity.

ORIGINAL WEALTH

God's original design for wealth was revealed in the garden of Eden. Everything good flourished for the enjoyment of humans. It was a picture of great wealth since there was no lack of anything. God's design was for humans to work and to take care of God's garden.

But sin entered the garden, and people chose to abandon God's original design. The fall of humankind perverted wealth as brokenness entered the world. Selfishness, greed, and disobedience ensued.

God's design has always included the privilege of living eternally with Him in a kingdom of true wealth. "Blessed are those who fear the LORD, who find great delight in his commands… Wealth and riches are in their houses, and their righteousness endures forever" (Psalm 112:1, 3 NIV). And God's design for wealth doesn't include trouble. "The blessing of the LORD makes rich, and he adds no sorrow with it" (Proverbs 10:22). To have wealth without the trouble and sorrow that frequently accompany it, we need to view and treat it as God designed, which includes honoring Him with it. We want to honor God with all He has given us, using our resources in ways that bring pleasure to Him and cause no shame for us when we give an accounting of our time, talent, and treasure.

WEALTHY PEOPLE IN MODERN TIMES

God has used extremely wealthy people in modern times for His purposes.

Andrew Carnegie built an enormous industry now known as U.S. Steel. Early in his life, his Christian mother heavily influenced the young Carnegie, who later "worked tirelessly to give his fortune away to benefit the less fortunate."[1] As a philanthropist, "the capitalist dedicated much of his restless energy to good works. His 1889 essay 'The Gospel of Wealth' charged industrial capitalists with the social responsibility to redistribute their fortunes in order to create opportunities for the worthy poor."[2] Carnegie built more than two thousand public libraries, including one in my hometown. He endowed universities, provided teacher pensions, funded scholarships, and even funded

---

1   Philip F. Anschutz, *Out Where the West Begins* (Denver, CO: Cloud Camp Press, 2017), 293.

2   Anschutz, *Out Where the West Begins*, 299.

the Peace Palace in The Hague, Netherlands, known today as the International Court of Justice. He set up the Carnegie Corporation to distribute 90 percent of his fortune to worthy causes.[3]

Bunker Hunt, the son of an oil baron, funded the development of the *Jesus* film produced by Campus Crusade for Christ in 1979. This film has been the most widely used evangelistic tool throughout the world over the past forty years. As of 2023, it's been shown in over two thousand languages for literally billions of people to see the life of Jesus portrayed in a movie.[4] What an incredible gift to God's kingdom! When wealth is deployed into the kingdom by wealthy men and women, God's purposes for His blessing are fulfilled.

RICH PEOPLE IN THE BIBLE

Throughout the course of history, God has used wealthy people for His purposes in the kingdom. In one of the earliest stories in the Bible, Job was recognized as a faithful steward of life and possessions. Through adversity and testing allowed by God, he lost his great wealth and children. Because Job remained faithful to God through perseverance, God restored Job's wealth to him. He may well have been one of the wealthiest men on earth.

Abraham, the father of the Jewish nation, was wealthy and obedient to God's calling and direction for his wealth. King David and his son Solomon became wealthy beyond earthly comparison as they ruled their kingdoms. Most importantly, David sought the Lord's pleasure and loved God more than his own wealth. He must have realized that God had given him his wealth for purposes greater than his own consumption.

---

3   Anschutz, *Out Where the West Begins*, 299.

4   "Jesus Film Project Ministry Statistics," Jesus Film Project, accessed November 7, 2023, https://www.jesusfilm.org/partners/resources/strategies/statistics/.

The New Testament notes how God used rich people. Some of these include the following:

1. Matthew (Levi), the tax collector who became the apostle who wrote the gospel of Matthew
2. A rich young ruler
3. Zacchaeus, a tax collector
4. The owner of the home where the last supper was held
5. Nicodemus, the Pharisee who sought after Jesus and later helped with his burial
6. Joseph of Arimathea, who asked Pilate for Jesus' body for burial
7. Barnabas, landowner and companion of the apostle Paul
8. Theophilus, who commissioned Luke to write the books of Luke and Acts

Let's look more closely at how the New Testament describes these people and see what lessons we can learn from their lives and use of their wealth.

A RICH YOUNG RULER

In the gospel of Mark, a rich young man asked Jesus how to inherit eternal life. "As Jesus started on his way, a man ran up to him and fell on his knees before him. 'Good teacher,' he asked, 'what must I do to inherit eternal life?'" (10:17 NIV). Notice that he fell on his knees imploring the Lord to answer his important question.

Jesus' initial answer was for the young man to follow the commandments (v. 19). Like many of us, the young man had rationalized his self-righteousness to the point that he could sincerely answer, "All these I have kept since I was a boy" (v. 20 NIV).

This prompted Jesus to reveal the man's heart. After all, "Jesus looked at him and loved him" (v. 21 NIV). Isn't that

interesting? Jesus was about to issue a very difficult requirement—one that He knew would be refused—and looked upon
this man with affection. I speculate that the young man may have
become rich as a result of following God's principles since God
grants wealth to whom He desires. Clearly, Jesus is not there to
condemn him but to offer him the best possible opportunity.

One simple direction was all it took to expose the man's
heart. "Go, sell everything you have and give to the poor, and
you will have treasure in heaven. Then come, follow me" (v. 21
NIV). Although I don't know what the man expected to hear, I'm
pretty sure it wasn't this challenge.

Now, we're not sure what happened to this young man
after he walked away "sorrowful" (v. 22). Jesus did not ask him
to become poor but simply to give away his possessions. This
young ruler went away thinking about the decision of a lifetime,
an invitation that was actually a request for his heart. Total commitment is not a money issue; it's a heart issue. Put yourself in
his position. If you were asked today to put everything on the
table, everything of value, and give it for the sake of Christ and
His kingdom, would you be willing to do it?

A TAX COLLECTOR

Jesus encountered another rich man on His way to Jerusalem.
As He was passing through Jericho, He met a wealthy chief tax
collector who was earnestly seeking after Him. "A man was there
by the name of Zacchaeus; he was a chief tax collector and was
wealthy. He wanted to see who Jesus was, but because he was
short he could not see over the crowd. So he ran ahead and
climbed a sycamore-fig tree to see him, since Jesus was coming
that way" (Luke 19:2–4 NIV).

Approaching Zacchaeus' perch in the tree, Jesus looked up
and called him by name. Zacchaeus scrambled down and greeted
Jesus joyfully, taking Him to his home. Once there, as a result of

his repentant heart, salvation came to Zacchaeus and his household. He put his faith into action by giving half of his possessions to the poor and making restitution for his misdeeds with a 400 percent refund. By tearing his heart away from money, he was able to follow Christ.

A HOMEOWNER

Another rich man we know little about provided the house for the Passover Feast on the night before the crucifixion. Jesus asked Peter and John to go prepare for the Passover—without them having any idea that this would be their final dinner together. We know it happened in a rich man's house because he had servants and a large upper room with all the furnishings. Although we have no personal details regarding the homeowner, it is apparent that he was available, had margin in his life, and offered the assets with which God had blessed him.

A RICH MAN'S TOMB

God used Joseph of Arimathea, another rich man, to properly bury His Son, Jesus. We read of this beautiful act in Matthew 27:57–60. "When it was evening, there came a rich man from Arimathea, named Joseph, who also was a disciple of Jesus. He went to Pilate and asked for the body of Jesus…And Joseph took the body and wrapped it in a clean linen shroud and laid it in his own new tomb, which he had cut in the rock."

Joseph's wealth and status certainly contributed to his influence and ability to approach Pontius Pilate with his request for Jesus' body. Without financial means, the ordinary disciple would not likely have had the opportunity to make the request, much less have it granted. Joseph of Arimathea used both his physical and nonphysical wealth to honor Jesus with a temporary earthly resting place.

THREE RICH, POOR WOMEN

Wealth in God's kingdom is upside down to the world's value system. During biblical times, women were treated as second-class citizens, yet Jesus honored women—common women—and used their example for us to follow in our stewardship journey. In learning the stories of these women, I realized four things: (1) the amount of money is not the primary issue in God's kingdom; (2) my generosity should be extravagant; (3) God, who doesn't need my money, desires my heart and knows how tied it is to my money; and (4) He wants me to experience the complete security found only in Him.

In the spirit of faithfulness, a poor widow quietly went up to the temple and placed an offering of two small copper coins in the temple treasury. Jesus noticed.

Think of the implications for a moment: Jesus noticed. How important is that?

Then He immortalized her in Scripture by saying that she gave more than all the others. By kingdom standards, no one could have given more. It was the total of her earthly security, all she had to live on. Although the physical amount was tiny, less than one percent of a day's wage, the spiritual amount was beyond calculation. This quiet act of faith, done with no clue that the Son of God was watching, took enormous courage and trust.

Then there is the account of a woman who anointed Jesus with the alabaster jar of expensive perfume. Few examples can match this extravagant generosity. All four Gospels tell of a woman anointing Jesus, with one of them saying that the perfume cost a year's wage, probably around $20,000 in current value. One account shows the woman breaking the flask so that it could not be used again. She poured the perfume over Jesus' head while He reclined at dinner, anointing His body before a pending burial that she could not have known was imminent.

Unaware of its historic significance, her extreme generosity was an act of worship now known to all.

Another woman, broken and known for her sin, performed an extraordinary act of humility. In deep gratitude, she wept at the feet of Jesus, wiping His feet with her hair after soaking them with her tears. Anointing and kissing His feet was an act of worship that required shameless abandon in the presence of self-righteous critics.

These women gave their hearts and resources to honor the Lord. Whether the amount was two small coins or a year's wage of extremely expensive perfume, the common denominator was the heart of the faithful, generous, and humble steward. These women gave everything to Jesus. This was truly upside down to their world then—and to our world today.

When we look at these women as examples, we see that they made everything available for the kingdom. Nothing was saved, stashed, hoarded, or even "stewarded" for retirement. Giving it all demonstrated their total dedication.

IT'S OKAY TO HAVE WEALTH

Wealth is actually good. As Proverbs tells us, "In the house of the righteous there is much treasure" (15:6). The person who fears the Lord and delights in His commandments may well have wealth and riches in their house, along with righteousness that endures forever (Psalm 112:3). Righteous wealth—used properly—will last forever.

Just think of the power of the man or woman who uses their wealth as directed by God. Wealth in the hands of a steward is a powerful thing. It's okay to be rich in this world. It will be even better in the world to come.

Chapter 3

STEWARDSHIP IS A JOURNEY

Stewardship is a journey that lasts for eternity. Christ's parables often mention future additional responsibilities as a reward for earthly stewardship. Matthew 25:21 is one example: "His master said to him, 'Well done, good and faithful servant. You have been faithful over a little; I will set you over much. Enter into the joy of your master.'" God uses our stewardship as a training ground for righteous character and to develop our eternal significance.

DEFINING A STEWARD

The faithful steward takes care of his master's people and possessions. We see this in the parable Jesus taught in Luke 12:35–40. He further describes a good steward in Luke 12:41–48. The faithful and wise manager consistently performed his duties as instructed regardless of how long the master delayed his return or at what unexpected time he came. The master was always watching and always ready to reward faithful stewards. In this case, Jesus said that the master "will set him over all his possessions" (v. 44).

The journey of becoming a steward often has four distinctive phases. In my life, these phases have had much to do with my attitude toward giving and have been more philosophical than chronological.

In the first phase of my journey, I learned to become a *giver* to the Lord's work. Early in my life as a young Christian, I began to see the importance of simply giving money for the cause of Christ. The tithe is certainly a great place to start, but it is not the best place to end. As tithers, we begin to release ourselves from the love of our possessions. Since I was not naturally generous, just being able to give money at all was a big first step. As newlyweds, Marydel and I gave a large monetary wedding gift to the church. This initial act of giving was a major step of faith for us.

Another phase of my journey involved giving larger sums of money and becoming a *generous giver*. Let me qualify the "larger sums" by saying that generosity is less about size and more about attitude and proportion of income. As the proportion of giving to income grew, so did the development of an investment mentality. And it didn't stop with money; my wife and I also became involved with ministries we invested in. We were discovering in our personal experience the truth of Matthew 6:21: "For where your treasure is, there your heart will be also." Being a generous giver has occupied much of our stewardship journey.

I'll call the next phase *sacrificial giver*, although I'm not so sure we have ever given sacrificially. In other words, we haven't given to the point that we had to do without. It doesn't mean that we haven't given significant amounts; it just means that we have not truly had to sacrifice because of it. I have met others, though, who do give sacrificially. It might involve small sums of money because their funds are limited to begin with. So although I include sacrificial giver as a phase in the journey to stewardship, it's not one I lay claim to personally.

The final phase for me was learning what it means to become a *steward*. This came from the revelation that God actually owns all my assets and that I am simply a manager of what He entrusts to me. This flips the entire picture of giving. More than just a question of what portion of my income I give to Him, it becomes a question of what I will hold back for my personal use as I distribute the rest at His discretion. It's not just about what we give; it's also about what we consume. The moment I realized that "my possessions" were only mine to manage as God directed was the moment my journey progressed to stewardship.

Another part of the stewardship journey is working with other faithful, kingdom-minded leaders. The idea of effective stewardship has led us to believe that stewardship involves entrusting financial assets to other faithful people, who will in turn steward within their own ministry's projects and businesses. Investing in other stewards takes knowledge, skill, and accountability. It is both difficult and time consuming to find other effective and successful stewards with whom to partner in kingdom investments. But I think the Bible provides convincing evidence that entrusting wealth to other stewards is the best way to make a long-term impact.

God has designed all resources to be used in His kingdom. In other words, we should not withhold anything we possess. Is there anything so precious to us that we would keep it from Jesus?

THE DISCIPLINE OF A STEWARD

Discipline is required to be a successful steward in God's kingdom. The discipline of stewardship is a decision of the will, similar to the decision to follow Jesus Christ. Jesus invites us to follow him, just as he invited His disciples, Zacchaeus, and the rich young ruler.

The decision to become a steward requires simple obedience. As a steward, you are in the service of the Master, owning nothing but the privilege of managing the Master's affairs. When God entrusts money to us, I think He's looking for a return. If we are found faithful, He entrusts additional assets to our care. I believe God is in the business of making profits through His stewards.

The discipline of stewardship is like any other discipline. Obedience to God doesn't come naturally in this present world. We must exercise our obedience much like athletes train their body to obey the commands of their mind.

Several years ago, Marydel and I wanted to give money to International Justice Mission (IJM). We wanted to help free enslaved people and fight exploitation in third-world countries. We felt impressed by God to redeem a retirement annuity and give it to the ministry for their use in combating these atrocities. Since redeeming the annuity would require paying regular income taxes on all the gains, we were advised against it. The advice was to avoid paying taxes by holding the annuity until death and then letting our estate distribute it tax-free. But we felt a sense of urgency and didn't want to wait until our death to transfer this money to IJM. So we redeemed the annuity, paid the income tax on the gain, and gave the balance to IJM for their use. We knew that God could multiply the immediate gift far more than the tax savings that would accrue over the long delay.

If we truly believe God owns the world and everything in it (Psalm 50:10–12) and if we believe the parable of the talents (Matthew 25:14–30), we logically conclude that God funds His work through faithful stewards, that we are conduits for His work.

STEWARDSHIP IS BEARING FRUIT BY JOYFUL WORK

John the Baptist said every tree "that does not bear good fruit is cut down and thrown into the fire" (Luke 3:9). John explained that the tree is given the opportunity to produce fruit. God allows it to grow by watering it through rain and nourishing it through the soil. As the tree grows, it has every opportunity to bear fruit. If it doesn't, its purpose is not realized. Good stewardship requires this unfruitful tree to be cut down to make room for another tree that *will* fulfill its purpose. In the same way, God created us to bear fruit in His kingdom. It is sobering to think of the consequences of not bearing fruit.

Jesus made it clear that we are recognized by our fruit. In Matthew 7:17–20, He said, "Every healthy tree bears good fruit, but the diseased tree bears bad fruit. A healthy tree cannot bear bad fruit, nor can a diseased tree bear good fruit. Every tree that does not bear good fruit is cut down and thrown into the fire. Thus you will recognize them by their fruits."

Good works are a key to stewardship. When we share with those in need and do not keep everything for ourselves, we exercise good stewardship. God's purpose for blessing us is to enable us to bless others. This means taking action, actually doing what Jesus directs us to do as we stand in His place as His stewards.

The apostle James emphasizes that words, feelings, and even faith do not equal the fruit we are called to produce. "What good is it, my brothers, if someone says he has faith but does not have works? Can that faith save him? If a brother or sister is poorly clothed and lacking in daily food, and one of you says to them, 'Go in peace, be warmed and filled,' without giving them the things needed for the body, what good is that? So also faith by itself, if it does not have works, is dead" (James 2:14–17). Faith that really matters is proven to be alive through the good works—the fruit— it produces. This requires exercising our faith in a visual, tangible way by working hard in the kingdom. Although faith generally precedes our works, if it is not demonstrated through our works, our faith reveals itself to be dead, powerless, and meaningless.

I want this next sentence to be a profound encouragement to you; please think carefully about how it applies to your past experience and current circumstances: not everything you do will be successful, but everything you do in faith will bear the fruit of righteousness and will develop your character as a steward.

We know that God causes all things to work together for good, particularly for those who love the Lord and are diligently working to walk by faith. We are to be joyful in our hard work so that both our effort and our attitude will please the Master when we stand before Him. Think of employees you have seen. When they are lethargic and lazy in their assigned tasks, their employer becomes frustrated and maybe even angry. If human employers know the value of doing a job with joy, enthusiasm, and gratitude, how much more do you think the Lord wants that for us as we work to bear fruit for Him?

THE NUDGING OF THE HOLY SPIRIT

While in college, I wanted to work in Myrtle Beach, South Carolina, for a summer beach project with Campus Crusade for Christ (now called Cru). This summer project required each of us to work full-time jobs during the week and conduct ministry events during the evenings and weekends. We were to be self-supporting and sustainable through our employment. Wanting to find a job in my anticipated profession, I looked for a summer internship with an architectural firm.

I sent out many letters requesting interviews with firms in that area. Rejected by most, I became discouraged. This discouragement was aggravated when one of the letters I had sent was returned because of an improper address. "What's the use?" I mumbled, tossing the returned letter in the trash. But something deep inside prompted me to find the proper address and resend the letter. So despite my discouragement, I did just that. You've probably already guessed what happened: that very firm was the one that replied with a job offer for the summer. Despite being so close to giving up, God's Spirit nudged me to keep plodding forward. I am extremely grateful for His personal care.

I didn't realize until later how important it was to obey what I believed was God's direction. By obeying the Holy Spirit, I used my time that summer to advance God's kingdom. Not only did I experience a wonderful internship for the summer, but I was also blessed by long-term relationships with my new architect friends. They were instrumental in my development and a great kickoff to my architectural career.

NAVY SEALS DON'T MARCH IN THE PARADE

Jesus gives us yet another lesson in how God's kingdom differs from our natural desires.

> Beware of practicing your righteousness before other people in order to be seen by them, for then you will have no reward from your Father who is in heaven.
>
> Thus, when you give to the needy, sound no trumpet before you, as the hypocrites do in the synagogues and in the streets, that they may be praised by others. Truly, I say to you, they have received their reward. (Matthew 6:1–2)

To receive future rewards in heaven—and a much stronger commendation—our giving must be done with God as our audience of One. This call to secrecy is a key part of the stewardship journey because it protects us from the natural temptation to give for show, which risks receiving our only credit from others on earth rather than from God.

I've never been a fan of the hypocrites Jesus described. Navy SEALs, on the other hand, have always fascinated and impressed me. Although they are the elite group called upon for critical missions, they don't talk much about themselves. In fact, they don't usually even tell you that they are (or were) a Navy SEAL. But they know each other and are bonded in a close brotherhood of mutual respect.

My knowledge of what it's like to be a SEAL is not from firsthand experience but from several friends and a cousin who have served as Navy SEALs. They don't talk about their exploits, but they are self-assured in a confidence-inspiring way. Most missions are secret, and I'm sure tradition requires them to keep a lid on what they did. I admire their restraint and humility in front of others, their refusal to seek or need credit for what they do.

I have never noticed a Navy SEAL marching in a parade. Their role isn't public relations. It's to do the tough jobs that require skill, courage, and the willingness to put their own safety at the back of the priority line. When they perform according to plan, nobody sees them, but something definitely changes. Well-equipped and extensively trained prior to their missions, they work with confidence because they are so well prepared. These same attributes should define our work in God's kingdom, especially in hostile environments. Ministries should be consistently earning a reputation for being well supplied before they embark, working effectively with others, making a significant difference, and not grasping for credit. All these enhance mission success.

I want to be like the Navy SEALs in God's kingdom. I want to come and go free of the burdens and temptations of public acclaim. Whether anyone else knows it or not, I know I have been in action. The one thing I *do* want everyone around to know is that something changed. For the better. I want a long line of successful missions, but I don't want the medals to prove it. Not yet.

Chapter 4

GOD REDEEMS BROKEN PEOPLE

IMPERFECT MEN AND WOMEN

Stewardship is developed through obedience to the Holy Spirit. Because of our natural resistance to obey, our sinful nature can dominate. Brokenness can loosen the hold of pride and arrogance that causes our resistance to God's direction for our lives.

God uses imperfect but redeemed men and women to accomplish His purposes on earth. A lack of perfection does not disqualify someone. Although God would certainly use perfect people, He can't because they don't exist. We all sin, but those who confess and repent are useful to God; they are obedient at the right time.

Throughout history we see the pattern. Look at the life of Peter. Many times he acknowledged that Christ was the Messiah, but at two critical points in Jesus' life, Peter abandoned Him. Three times he fell asleep in the garden of Gethsemane despite Jesus' pleas to watch and pray. Then he denied knowing Jesus at His most critical hour while on trial for crimes He did not commit. Peter later went back to fishing, and Jesus had to recall him to his purpose as the shepherd of His church. Because Peter always recovered and returned to obedience, Jesus relied on him as the rock upon whom He would build His church.

God uses broken men and women. I believe that God cannot fully utilize someone until that person has been broken of their prideful selfishness and submits to God's authority over them. My dear friend Howard Dayton personally told me that brokenness comes in two ways: "You can either be broken by God through His Word or through your own circumstances. It's always best to be broken through the Word."

BROKENNESS

Some people know they are broken. I would much rather hang with people who admit their brokenness than those who look good but are hiding something. I know both kinds well because I have *been* both. Pride has crept in, searing my senses and my conscience. This searing invaded my soul and dulled my sensitivity, disrupting my intimate communion with God.

Several times I've had to ask the Lord to break me of the arrogance that cripples my fellowship with Him. I could sense that I was not following Him by walking in the Spirit. But after I had endured the pain of brokenness, He helped me tune my senses to better focus on the important things around me. As a bonus, He even enabled me to experience colors more vividly and smells more fragrantly than before.

Sometimes sin causes irreparable damage. Continual sin leads to a searing of the soul: a branding and scarring that may remain. Because the consequences of sin seem to vary greatly, we logically conclude that there is a difference in seriousness of sin. And there *is* a difference in the horizontal sense of our sins against each other. Some have consequences far worse than others. But in the vertical sense of our sins against God, even the least is damaging because of the barrier it places between us and Him. All sin breaks intimate fellowship with God and affects those we love. The consequence of our sin is much like the breaking of pottery; it might be fixed, but the value is forever altered.

I don't like going through brokenness caused by sin. Who does? But by God's grace, it was in that brokenness that I desperately began to seek the Lord with my whole heart. I began to abide with Him, restoring our fellowship. Coming out the other side of brokenness is a beautiful thing. It's a journey from weak and sin-sick to broken and sidelined to redeemed and restored to become useful again. God can heal a seared heart, and the senses can again come alive and enjoy intimate fellowship with God. "I will give you a new heart, and a new spirit I will put within you. And I will remove the heart of stone from your flesh and give you a heart of flesh" (Ezekiel 36:26).

GOD USES FLAWED PEOPLE

Brokenness seems to help people realize their failings and sinfulness. Throughout the New Testament, God called broken men and women to follow Him. The broken, realizing their frailty, may struggle with low self-esteem, but God delights in raising them to do great things as they rely completely on His power.

My dear friend John Enright, whose story I told in the first chapter, had followed in his parents' footsteps as a missionary most of his life. Somewhere along the way, God's Word seemed to grab hold of him and break him. Although by nature John could be a proud man, getting a glimpse of the awesomeness of God's kingdom humbled him.

From the moment I first met John, I realized that he was different. Hearing him talk about what God wanted him to do for the poorest people in Africa, I sensed a certain humility about him. But this humility did nothing to undermine his confidence in what God had called him to do. Instead, it drove him to dedicate his life of leadership to serving the poor by building businesses through which they could flourish.

Years ago I met a businessman who built an orphanage in another part of Africa. He did great things because he heard the Holy Spirit urging him to do something about poor children living in dangerous slums. He wanted to bring deliverance and redemption from the atrocities they suffered. Unfortunately, even in a noble cause, success can open a door to pride and the undoing of many, as it did with my friend. Although broken he was still useful in God's kingdom because of his obedience to God's call to action.

But God can redeem anyone despite their prideful arrogance if they will only repent and again follow Him. We sometimes think we can accomplish great things for God, but the reality is that God uses us as servants to create His own kingdom. We must never forget that only God can make us successful.

RICH PEOPLE MUST WALK THROUGH BROKENNESS

I have come to believe that the Lord *must* break every person He intends to use.

Recent years have brought two great periods of brokenness in my life. The first came with my son when he was in high school. He was an outstanding young man, yet I sensed that he did not walk closely with the Lord. I simply asked God to break him so that he would be totally submitted to the Lord. What I didn't know at the time is that God would honor this request by breaking both of us. He knew that we both needed it in order to grow into the type of men He could use.

The second period of brokenness involved my relationship with my wife. I realized that in my pride and arrogance, I was not loving my wife unconditionally. My love for her was often conditional, based on what she did for me or how I felt about myself. This led me to do things that severely affected our family, things

I now regret. But during this time God broke me, along with my family, which then allowed all of us to focus more on His redemptive purpose in each of our lives. This brokenness forced me to cling to the Lord, to abide in Him as I never had before.

Most people who take an effective stand for the kingdom become a target for the Enemy. He exploits their vulnerabilities, making their weaknesses a focal point of his attack. I'm not sure how this can be avoided except through diligently abiding in God through obedience, spending time with the Lord in prayer and meditation, and staying regularly connected to an intimate group of brothers or sisters that holds us accountable. Although this kind of accountability involves judgment with love, it is not the kind of judgment that leads to condemnation. Its goal is to help us realign with truth so we can experience the healing and restoration we all need.

King David of the Old Testament—despite his intimate relationship with God—committed sins of great consequence. After being used by God in multiple miracles, including the slaying of Goliath and mighty battle victories, he did the inexcusable: he committed adultery and had the woman's husband killed (2 Samuel 11). (Even as I call it out as inexcusable, I'm struck by my tendency to grasp at a-dime-a-dozen excuses when I'm the guilty one.) Was it avoidable? I'm sure it was. Did he get away with it? Definitely not. But God found a way to use it in David's life to bring him closer. What David eventually realized was that a humble and contrite heart is what God wants.

As rich men and women, we all are likely to be a mess. Because the rich are given great resources, they are likely to become prime targets of pride and Satan's attacks. Fortunately, our God is redemptive and able to use them in His kingdom when they return to obedience.

A WILD HORSE

Brokenness, an essential element in anyone's journey of stewardship, leads us to total submission, like the taming of a wild horse. In the old days, cowboys would capture horses in the wild and bring them into the corral to be broken. A stallion might be a magnificent horse in the wild, but it isn't of much use to a cowboy until it is broken and submits its will to the rider.

A cowboy would corral a horse and then begin the breaking process. This meant a wild ride for the cowboy while the horse bucked and twisted in its unwillingness to submit. Finally, the horse would tire, and the cowboy could bring it under control. Once the horse's will was broken and it fully submitted to the rider, it became useful and enjoyed a new life of partnership with a caring master.

Although breaking is usually a one-time event, the horse regularly needs to be bridled to sense its master's direction. This bridling is a reminder of continual submission, similar to our ongoing decision to submit to the authority of Christ and yield to His leadership. Our obedience is not reserved for when it's convenient; it is to be complete and unconditional. We are reminded of this daily through our equivalent of the bridling process—the Word of God that continues to direct us by communicating His loving guidance. Just as an unbridled horse, even after it's broken, is useless to a cowboy, we are useless as stewards without daily affirmation of submission and obedience. How else can a steward become obedient to the prompting of the Lord?

BEING HONEST WITH MYSELF

We intuitively know that we need to be honest—with ourselves and about ourselves—if we want to serve God effectively. The problem is that we are nearly always self-deceived to some degree, even when we are sincerely trying to evaluate our strengths, our weaknesses, and especially our level of obedience. We typically rationalize and excuse ourselves for the very things we would see as obvious deficiencies in someone else.

Two biblical people best represent my life. I relate well to the rich young ruler and the apostle Peter. Very little is known about the rich young ruler. We know substantially more about Peter: his bold talk, his inconsistent walk, and his extreme devotion and passion for the Lord. Both men were flawed but important to Jesus. And they contributed to the good news of the gospel.

During much of my business and financial life I struggled like this rich young ruler. He is immortalized in Scripture because of his struggle with possessions. I relate to him because it took me quite a while to decide to give everything and follow Jesus.

I identify with Peter due to my own inconsistent walk with the Lord and sometimes indecisiveness to follow him closely. My emotions toss me like the waves, yet I desire to come back into the boat after attempting to walk on water toward Jesus.

THE BATTLE FOR YOUR HEART

I am a righteous man only because Christ has redeemed my heart of stone and given me His righteousness in exchange for my sin. Although I do good works in His kingdom and I love God, my old nature is still to sin.

I realize that goodness and evil dwell within the same heart, but it's a mystery I have difficulty understanding. I once thought that evil could not coexist in a redeemed heart, but that idea just doesn't match my experience. Although I don't understand how evil and goodness dwell simultaneously, I know that when I spend time with God, the fruit of the good and righteous heart develops. As the fruit develops, good dominates. But there is still a constant battle due to my sin nature, even though Christ has redeemed my heart.

This battle has caused me to do things that don't make sense. I've come to believe that everyone's heart is a battlefield. While reading the biblical parable of the weeds that were sown into the good field (Matthew 13:24–30), I began to understand this dilemma.

In this parable, Jesus told the audience that an enemy had come and sown weeds among the good wheat in a farmer's field. Good wheat and bad weeds began to grow together in an undesirable mix. The master told the confused servants to let both grow until harvest. When the wheat was ready for harvest, they should pull and burn the weeds first and then gather the wheat into the barn. One truth I draw from this is that the coexistence of good and evil in our heart doesn't mean that our heart is totally bad; the weeds just need to be removed.

The apostle Peter's confession about Jesus illustrates the battle for a heart: "'You are the Christ, the Son of the living God.' And Jesus answered him, 'Blessed are you, Simon Bar-Jonah! For flesh and blood has not revealed this to you, but my Father who is in heaven'" (Matthew 16:16–17). In this round, Peter's good heart got an A. But he failed the next test. Not long after this confession, Peter's heart was torn when Jesus revealed His imminent crucifixion. Peter responded, "'Far be it from you, Lord! This shall never happen to you!' But he turned and said to Peter, 'Get behind me, Satan! You are a hindrance to me. For you are not setting your mind on the things of God, but on the things of man'" (vv. 22–23).

Peter's inconsistency reflects the great struggle for his heart. Both good and evil were battling over Peter as God revealed truth to him and Satan worked to distort it. We know eventually that goodness won out because the keys of the kingdom of heaven were given to Peter and the Christian church was built upon his faithfulness.

The apostle Paul's heart also battled with good and evil. He wrote, "Although I want to do good, evil is right there with me. For in my inner being I delight in God's law; but I see another law at work in me, waging war against the law of my mind and making me a prisoner of the law of sin at work within me. What a wretched man I am! Who will rescue me from this body that is subject to death? Thanks be to God, who delivers me through Jesus Christ our Lord!" (Romans 7:21–25 NIV). The battles that raged in the hearts of Peter and Paul are the same that rage in our hearts today. Thank God we have the same ultimate victory through Jesus Christ.

Evil thoughts and perversions that defile us come out of our heart. "Out of the heart come evil thoughts, murder, adultery, sexual immorality, theft, false witness, slander. These are what defile a person" (Matthew 15:19–20). As a defense, we store up God's Word in our heart so we might not sin against Him (Psalm 119:11). The heart of a person stores good treasures that are expressed in what we say. I can now reconcile that the goodness Jesus brings into my heart as Savior and Lord will win out, just as the wheat was preserved in the parable of the weeds.

Many unseen spiritual forces battle in the war for the heart. As in any war, some battles are won and others lost, but each is unique. In this struggle between good and evil, there are casualties. Some lead to death, but most are wounds that eventually heal. God uses our sacrifices and injuries to advance His kingdom against the Enemy.

I wrestled in junior high and high school. Through extensive training and repetitive practice, I learned various wrestling holds, moves, and escapes. With each opponent's move, there was a reaction or countermove. No wrestler can afford to waste time thinking through a list of options during a match; the appropriate choice needs to become an automatic reaction. And eventually it did but not until I had spent a lot of time perfecting these strategies. Good habits develop from diligent training. In the same way, applying God's principles must become automatic habits deeply ingrained in my heart. When I abide with Christ by spending time with Him, He arms me for victories of the heart.

REDEMPTION VERSUS PERFECTION

I've had two horrifying experiences with my eighteen-month-old grandsons. Both involved water: one in our swimming pool and one at a lake. I was enjoying every moment of Will's delight as he toddled along the edge of our swimming pool. But in a split second I will never forget, he twirled around and fell into the water. Because I was so close, I was able to grab him immediately and pull him out of danger. In the other case, Ryder was playing along the water's edge at a mountain lake. We were standing right there with him while he jumped and splashed with joy. Suddenly, he was face down in the water. Again, because I was standing right there, I was able to jump in and grab him, pulling him to safety.

After-the-fact accounts of past incidents like these may sound tame or even routine, but in both cases, the stakes were as high as they could be—the life or death of my precious grandsons. Adrenaline propelled me into action that kept my heart pounding for many minutes as I thought of what could have happened if we had not been so close. Life is fragile.

These two incidents within a short span of time drove me to wonder about how I could continue to protect my dear grandchildren. I couldn't be around all the time; no one could. There had to be a different way. It occurred to me that it's better to know how to swim than to expect to stay out of the water or rely on someone else if you should fall in. Eighteen months old may be too young to learn to swim, but I determined that they would be taught as soon as they were able.

But there is another application to be made. The responsibility of always protecting my grandchildren is much like trying to live a life of perfection. I would always need to be on my toes, constantly surveying the environment to make sure everything was safe. And when the impossible-to-anticipate should threaten, I might need superhuman strength and speed to save the day. But I don't have these attributes. I'm not perfect, and I'm not superhuman. Thank God that there is a better away. Like learning to swim, God's forgiveness through redemption provides recovery from the battle when we wander from protection.

I wish I could live a perfect life. I don't want to stop trying, but by God's grace, my failures are teaching me to be a broken, redeemed man clinging closely to the Lord. That is my true rescue. As much as I have tried to live a good, morally perfect life, it is just as impossible as protecting my grandchildren for the rest of their lives.

Despite all the times I've screwed up in life, God's redemption has always been there to rescue me. The cost? Simply submitting to the Lord's grace and forgiveness with the desire to repent and walk more closely with Him. I wear myself out trying to be a "good boy." By contrast I find peace in following Jesus closely. It changes my heart and protects me so that I don't rely on perfection and my own efforts. When I mess up, the certain hope of forgiveness enables me to repent and move forward with the desire to follow Him more closely.

I can lock our back door to keep my grandchildren from falling in the pool, or I can endeavor to teach them how to swim. Of course it's good to keep the back door locked, just as we should attempt to live a godly life. But it's not fail-safe. The perfect lock doesn't exist. Neither does living perfectly. What *does* exist—and is readily available to all of us—is restoration through God's perfect redemption.

Chapter 5

ADVICE FOR THE RICH

GOD-GIVEN WEALTH

Wealth is a gift God gives men and women. He also gives them the power to enjoy it. "Everyone also to whom God has given wealth and possessions and power to enjoy them, and to accept his lot and rejoice in his toil—this is the gift of God" (Ecclesiastes 5:19).

The apostle Paul encouraged the church by saying that God will make sure that grace abounds to them "so that having all sufficiency in all things at all times, you may abound in every good work" (2 Corinthians 9:8). They will be able to distribute freely to the poor, and His righteousness will be evident in them.

God, who metaphorically supplies the seed for us to sow in His kingdom, will "multiply your seed for sowing and increase the harvest of your righteousness" (2 Corinthians 9:10). It is important to thank God for this provision and for its growth. We are a small but significant part in the process of deploying God-given wealth for His intended use.

If you sow abundantly, you will reap abundantly. Conversely, riches kept will accrue to the detriment of their owner. If someone sows sparingly and keeps everything for himself, they will suffer at harvest time. Ecclesiastes 5:13 says, "There is a grievous evil that I have seen under the sun: riches were kept by their owner to his hurt."

CHASING WEALTH

Solomon underscored the inability of wealth to provide the security we think it promises. "Do not toil to acquire wealth; be discerning enough to desist. When your eyes light on it, it is gone, for suddenly it sprouts wings, flying like an eagle toward heaven" (Proverbs 23:4–5). Good things become meaningless if their value and influence end on earth. Because wealth is temporary, it can never give us eternal security, which is why placing our trust in it instead of God will lead to ruin. "See the man who would not make God his refuge, but trusted in the abundance of his riches and sought refuge in his own destruction!" (Psalm 52:7). Just as wealth is temporary, so are our own lives. "As for man, his days are like grass; he flourishes like a flower of the field; for the wind passes over it, and it is gone, and its place knows it no more" (Psalm 103:15–16). What a sobering thought! We should evaluate everything from an eternal perspective: How do my actions matter for eternity?

Jesus further explained the folly of chasing temporary wealth as he talked to His disciples one day. "What will it profit a man if he gains the whole world and forfeits his soul? Or what shall a man give in return for his soul? For the Son of Man is going to come with his angels in the glory of his Father, and then he will repay each person according to what he has done" (Matthew 16:26–27).

Jesus knew that human hearts are inherently selfish, filled with desire to accumulate without even understanding why.

People who have "gained the world," such as Steve Jobs, Tim Cook, Warren Buffet, Bill Gates, Sam Walton, Jeff Bezos, or Elon Musk, have been given their ability to generate wealth. Some of them probably recognize that fact and are grateful for it; others may be convinced that they gained it solely through their own efforts. When you think about these people and their legacies, you will realize some are generous, some have dysfunctional families, and some live in fear. Some have sold out to worldly standards and pleasures, compromising their morals in a rush to gain all the world has to offer.

Why do so many people keep their stuff until the very end? Why do ultrarich people strive for additional wealth when they have more than they can spend and can't take it with them into eternity? Some do it for sport or to inflate their egos. Some may not have an answer beyond "because I can." In many cases it is probably a fear that they won't have enough. For some it may be a desire to prove their worth or maintain a status that is dependent on opulence. For others, it may simply be an inordinate love of valuable possessions.

Very few think in terms of stewarding their goods to other faithful people while they are still alive. But the fact remains that we cannot take anything with us. The Bible makes this notion clear: "As he came from his mother's womb he shall go again, naked as he came, and shall take nothing for his toil that he may carry away in his hand" (Ecclesiastes 5:15), and "When he dies he will carry nothing away; his glory will not go down after him" (Psalm 49:17). Wealth in and of itself is certainly not wrong, but its purpose and use determine whether it is valuable for eternity.

JESUS' TEACHINGS WARN THE RICH

Jesus warned the rich when He said, "Woe to you who are rich, for you have received your consolation" (Luke 6:24). This was a warning—not a condemnation—for every rich person. Shortly after, He followed with the positive side of the equation, the encouragement to be generous with their wealth. "Give, and it will be given to you. Good measure, pressed down, shaken together, running over, will be put into your lap. For with the measure you use it will be measured back to you" (v. 38). This is a reinforcement of the Golden Rule, to do to others as you would have them do to you. It makes all the sense in the world, but it defies fallen human nature.

Why did Jesus give this warning followed by this instruction? He wanted to convince His listeners that they would be known for the fruit they produced. "The good person out of the good treasure of his heart produces good, and the evil person out of his evil treasure produces evil, for out of the abundance of the heart his mouth speaks" (v. 45). Jesus wanted the wealth of a person to produce good fruit. He wanted them to do good with the money that had been entrusted to them, which could only happen if their heart was good.

Even when we see good fruit, we need to remain alert. Jesus later warned about the deceitfulness of riches in the parable about the seeds sown in four different types of soils. The third soil was probably healthy because the seed began to grow. But thorns representing the riches and pleasures of life grew alongside and later choked the good seed so that its fruit never matured. Jesus was saying that although a person might develop some positive characteristics, an attachment to riches will keep them from producing true value. Again, this was a warning, not a condemnation. We need to ensure that the thorns of pleasure and riches don't crowd out the good that we can do with our wealth.

Reminding us to guard against the thorns of pleasure and riches, Jesus frequently taught the importance of choosing the right values, saying, "Take care, and be on your guard against all covetousness, for one's life does not consist in the abundance of his possessions" (Luke 12:15). Keeping our eyes focused on God is important in ensuring we're using our money as God designed.

All these warnings can be summarized by this: "Truly, I say to you, only with difficulty will a rich person enter the kingdom of heaven" (Matthew 19:23). Why? Because if your money is tied to your heart, an idol replaces God as your focal point. This makes it very difficult to give to those in need. You would think that if rich men and women have extra wealth, it should not be hard to let some go. Greed is often fueled by the sin of pride, but it can also result from fear and insecurity. In either case, it is a sin of the heart.

Jesus gave us these warnings because there will be a great accounting for those who have been given much in this life. "Everyone to whom much was given, of him much will be required, and from him to whom they entrusted much, they will demand the more" (v. 48). A solution to making wealth your idol is simply choosing to become generous. It relaxes our hands, tearing our grip from our money. This is one of the biggest challenges for any of us. It is also the beginning of true stewardship in God's kingdom.

RICH PEOPLE JESUS WARNED US ABOUT

Jesus warned us of a rich man in a story: "There was a rich man who was dressed in purple and fine linen and lived in luxury every day. At his gate was laid a beggar named Lazarus, covered with sores and longing to eat what fell from the rich man's table. Even the dogs came and licked his sores" (Luke 16:19–21 NIV). This rich man had no regard for the poor. Prideful and arrogant, he ignored Lazarus as he laid at the gate. Embodying the world's perspective regarding wealth, the man received his good things while he was alive. Although the writings of Moses and the prophets gave him ample opportunity to repent and enter the kingdom of God, his disregard for truth took him to hell.

In another parable, Jesus described a second rich man: a hoarder who thought only of himself.

The ground of a certain rich man yielded an abundant harvest. He thought to himself, "What shall I do? I have no place to store my crops."

Then he said, "This is what I'll do. I will tear down my barns and build bigger ones, and there I will store my surplus grain. And I'll say to myself, 'You have plenty of grain laid up for many years. Take life easy; eat, drink and be merry.'" (Luke 12:16–19 NIV)

Jesus described this rich farmer as a fool. God had given this man his good harvest. Now, although this rich man was blessed, he did not give God the credit for his prosperity. Rather than being generous with God's gifts, he determined to focus only on pleasure and how he could maximize his gain to live a life of leisure.

Today it would be said this way: "I'll set aside plenty for the future. In fact, I might just retire early so I can enjoy my prosperity. After all, I deserve it because I've worked hard and built such a good business. I think I may build a bigger home, take it easy, play golf every day, go on great vacations, and manage my investments to take really good care of me and my family."

Watch out! We need to be careful lest we ignore God's leading to serve others with what He has provided for us—especially when His provision includes riches. Jesus concluded that this rich man was not rich toward God and those on God's heart. This disregard ended in his premature death.

THE RICH ARE TO BE HUMBLE

Using wealth selfishly for pleasure and exorbitant consumption will have severe consequences. The apostle James warned rich men and women not to boast in their wealth and position but rather in the humility of the grace of God. Material riches are a fickle friend to the one who trusts in them. "Like a flower of the grass he will pass away. For the sun rises with its scorching heat and withers the grass; its flower falls, and its beauty perishes. So also will the rich man fade away in the midst of his pursuits" (James 1:10–11).

James later came down even stronger on the rich who do not use their wealth for kingdom purposes.

> Come now, you rich, weep and howl for the miseries that are coming upon you. Your riches have rotted and your garments are moth-eaten. Your gold and silver have corroded, and their corrosion will be evidence against you and will eat your flesh like fire. You have laid up treasure in the last days. Behold, the wages of the laborers who mowed your fields, which you kept back by fraud, are crying out against you, and the cries of the harvesters have reached the ears of the Lord of hosts. You have lived on the earth in luxury and in self-indulgence. You have fattened your hearts in a day of slaughter. (James 5:1–5)

Wealth that is improperly gained or used will rise up as condemning evidence when we are called to give account for our stewardship.

But there is also good news: those who use their wealth for God's kingdom will be greatly rewarded for honoring Him and His intended purpose for entrusting wealth to them. I'll tell you stories later of faithful men and women who humbly used their wealth to create economic engines to be used to further God's kingdom by employing many while sharing the gospel message.

WEALTH FOR GOD'S GLORY

Having wealth is certainly not wrong. God, who created everything, distributes wealth for His intended purposes to whomever

He chooses. The Bible condemns no one for merely being rich, but God is concerned with how wealth is used. Money is power that can be used to build His kingdom—on earth and for eternity. And that is a good thing.

As James said, "Every good gift and every perfect gift is from above, coming down from the Father of lights" (1:17). This includes wealth and our possessions. Since God gives only good gifts, and wealth is one of those, we should not feel guilt, shame, or pride about what we receive. Rather, we should welcome it along with the privilege of using it for God and His kingdom.

James is a very practical book, giving us valuable instruction for living out our faith. Think of how this verse alone would have given all the counsel needed for the two rich men Jesus warned us about. "If you really fulfill the royal law according to the Scripture, 'You shall love your neighbor as yourself,' you are doing well" (James 2:8). This golden thread of love runs throughout the tapestry of God's economy. If Lazarus' master and the rich farmer had followed it, it would have made all the difference for them.

Chapter 6

WHY WORK–REALLY?

WHY AM I HERE?

A question all men and women must answer for themselves is why they are here.

Most of us rarely take time to examine the most important questions of life. Having never paused to contemplate them, I realized that I needed to answer these foundational questions for myself.

1. What is my overall purpose and mission, and who am I to become?
2. Why am I in business to make profit, and how do I convert wealth into eternal treasure?

After college, I was so busy working and raising a family that these questions always fled in the face of more immediate ones. Later, I began wondering more about the meaning of life—particularly *my* life. Why had God put me here to work to begin with?

A lot was fuzzy, but one important idea emerged. God designed everything in my life to develop my character in keeping with His unique plan for me. Life's positive and negative experiences served as God's development strategy to prepare me for a good future that only He could see. Failures lay ahead because I needed a humble heart. Their price would be brokenness and, thanks to His grace, redemption. Only as a redeemed servant of His kingdom would I hear the soft voice of the loving Father and be still enough to discern the whispers of His Spirit.

Through life's experiences, I see five key components for my work in God's kingdom. They are (1) igniting kingdom businesses through investment, (2) encouraging key ministry leaders by bearing their burdens, (3) mentoring young leaders, (4) generously funding God's kingdom, and (5) applying business principles through running a profitable business and writing about it.

Zooming out to a slightly wider view, I see an important foundation upon which all five of these purposes must be built: compassionate love for my wife and family if I want to see God glorified through my efforts.

WHY TOIL?

Ecclesiastes is a wonderful Old Testament book written by King Solomon late in his life. As he reflected on his accomplishments on earth, he asked questions like these: What do people gain for all their toil under the sun? What good is it for people to work all their lives for something on this earth?

His answer seems to point to two benefits: enjoyment of the work itself and the enjoyment of acquiring things. But he also recognized that these did not bring lasting satisfaction. So his advice was to have joy in your work, give it all your energy, and enjoy life while you can. But then he adds a downer: nothing can be transported into eternity, and whatever you gain on this earth will be left to others.

Solomon knew that the Egyptian pharaohs were buried with their possessions, but he concluded that the strategy did them no good. We can say with authority that these possessions never made it to heaven. Just look at all the treasures uncovered by archeologists! Solomon's understanding that nothing goes with us when we die led him to label earthly efforts this way: "All is vanity" (Ecclesiastes 1:2).

So what was Solomon actually saying? That working hard could be of no avail or benefit since we will all die? Yes, in part, but there was also a hopeful, optimistic message that our work is for our own good. We were created to work and be productive. Our toil produces pleasure as we develop our God-given ability to be fruitful while we serve on earth.

But then Solomon went a step further, telling us that even though we cannot comprehend it, God has put a longing into our hearts. "He has also set eternity in the human heart; yet no one can fathom what God has done from beginning to end" (3:11 NIV).

We comprehend this concept more clearly from our New Testament perspective of eternity. We can rejoice in our work and have pleasure in everything we do on earth that aligns with our eternal purpose. Nothing done for God's kingdom simply dies with us. Nor is it ever in vain. His kingdom is eternal—as are our contributions to it.

Solomon's reflection on his life in Ecclesiastes seems a bit morbid. He often concluded that everything is meaningless. I would limit the "everything" to things like the pursuit of pleasure, leisure, physical wealth, and other items of only temporal value. Much of what Solomon did had eternal value. The wisdom he gained and the understanding he applied worked for his eternal benefit. And ours. Who can measure the benefit of the book of Proverbs, which he wrote most of? Consider the value of just this single verse: "Commit your work to the LORD, and your plans will be established" (Proverbs 16:3). A few verses later he shed light on how this works: "The heart of man plans his way, but the LORD establishes his steps" (v. 9).

Moses had previously prayed something that may seem unrelated, but I interpret it as part of a strategy to make sure our lives count for more than just the moment. He asked the Lord, "Teach us to number our days that we may get a heart of wisdom" (Psalm 90:12). This sounds to me like a request for awareness and realization that each day of our limited time on earth needs to contribute to our big-picture purpose.

So how will we know if our days are meaningless or if they have a deeper purpose? Some days we may think that our toil doesn't matter, but in reality, even small, mundane tasks are the building blocks of a life of eternal purpose. Let me illustrate with a baseball game.

A baseball player swings at a dozen or so pitches every game. If just one swing in every game turned out to be a home run, he would break every record in the book. Instead, many swings are misses, many are foul balls, and, based on batting averages, only one is likely to be a base hit of any kind. But they all work together for the baseball team to win the game. Our everyday work life is like a baseball game with strikeouts, walks, hits, and runs, but we value each day as a necessary part of the big picture: lifelong work of eternal value.

So why do we work? God created us for work, to find fulfillment in our toil. We are to work hard because that brings internal fulfillment and joy to our soul. Ephesians 2:10 gives us a great example of our purpose in working: "We are his workmanship, created in Christ Jesus for good works, which God prepared beforehand, that we should walk in them." By God's design, we should work with all our might, doing our work well and with enthusiasm and diligence. He rewards us with joy and meaning in the days He gives us on earth.

WORKING FOR SUCCESS

Most men and women in the workplace work hard to be successful. They pursue their careers hoping to accomplish and accumulate much. This is not a problem if the perspective is right. If, however, we view all our effort and accomplishments as a vapor that vanishes at our death, then we may work accordingly—and much of it *will* be wasted and not benefit us in eternity. But men and women who work with an eternal perspective realize that their wealth and accomplishments can be deposits in a life with no end. The same amount of effort but different motivation and focus yields an enormously better outcome.

I have not met many men and women who believe they are living in light of eternity, regardless of what they may say. If they really believed it, they would realize that everything they do is eternally important. We should minimize the time we spend on activities that don't amount to much in eternity. This doesn't mean we can't have fun or enjoy life. It means that eliminating some things will enable us to focus on others that yield greater fulfillment. Don't forget that some activities, like hobbies we love, can become a platform for meeting and ministering to people who need to see a reflection of Christ. An upgrade in the vision of our heart can transform a mere hobby into a life-changing personal ministry.

Doesn't it make more sense to work diligently for things that last for eternity rather than for things that will be useless and forgotten the moment we pass? Our lives on earth are only a speck against the backdrop of eternity. Isn't it logical then to work for the long-term value rather than settle for short-term pleasures, accomplishments, and accolades? Are you following the lesson of Solomon in Ecclesiastes, using your time wisely to build things that last? Anything else is shortsighted vanity, chasing after the wind.

Jesus Christ will judge our ultimate success when we stand before Him. This is great motivation to focus on lasting values, efforts that impact the eternal welfare of those God places in our sphere of influence.

A PURPOSE TO GENERATE PROFITS

After forty years in business, I learned to produce profit to build God's kingdom. These profits enabled me to take care of my family, employees, and others. Profit also allowed the people around me to flourish with prosperity.

I have wondered why the Lord took me on a journey of practicing architecture. I knew since college that I should be involved in ministry, but I didn't feel called to vocational ministry on a full-time basis. I originally thought my ministry would be completely separate from my vocational work as a professional. Have I been surprised! As an architect for these many years, God has been training me as a steward. These years helped me develop the discipline, skills, and resources I needed to be the steward He had designed and called me to be. It was all part of His training plan for me.

I am an investor in God's kingdom—a venture capitalist to build the kingdom on earth in preparing for eternity future. I am skilled in investing in people God has anointed, as the Holy Spirit shows them to me. I am only as successful as my obedience in following the Holy Spirit's nudging and directions. I have to listen, feeling these prompts spiritually. The Lord will show me where he wants his assets to be invested, deployed, and used. I must have his wisdom. God has not just called me to donate money for others to spend but to find stewards (of their portion of the kingdom) and empower them.

WHOSE WORK IS IT?

"May the favor of the Lord our God rest on us; establish the work of our hands for us—yes, establish the work of our hands" (Psalm 90:17 NIV).

We should be about the Lord's work. I interpret this verse to mean that we need to ask God what He wants us to do and then listen carefully. We frequently ask God to bless what we have independently decided to do, assuming that we are serving Him. But to truly serve Him is to respond to His leading, to pursue His agenda in the way that He has uniquely designed for us to fit in, and to reap a harvest. Success in God's kingdom is carefully listening to the Holy Spirit and obeying His whispers.

It often seems more appealing to do what we assume God wants, partly because it may be what *we* want disguised in church clothes. But sometimes we sincerely want to follow His lead, and we just have trouble identifying it. It's not easy to labor in prayer and then patiently listen for the Lord's whispers. But that is step one in being a faithful steward or manager of God's resources—including our own abilities and opportunities. We can be confident of God's favor when we listen carefully to and do His will.

WHAT AM I GIFTED TO DO WELL?

Sometimes I have become conflicted while working with business and ministry partners. This struggle has resulted from the perception that I had to help them based on my expertise in their field. But I am an architect. I have zero experience or knowledge of running a movie business. My involvement in foreign missions cannot be based on missiological knowledge because I don't possess it. I have not been called to be a movie director or a foreign missionary, but I know that I have been called to help those who are. So what am I equipped to do?

Once I discovered that I am gifted at doing certain things well, it gave me great freedom from discouragement and frustration. I am talented at helping others develop businesses by contributing capital, consulting, and sharing wisdom from experience. I love a statement attributed to Ross Perot: "I pick the jockeys, and the jockeys pick the horses and ride them."[5] I try to do that with the men and women I work with in God's kingdom. My lack of knowledge of their business or mission no longer hampers me. I can help them with my giftedness.

I have discovered that giftedness is what I can do that no one else can do as well. Okay, let me qualify that just a bit by adding the clause "in a given time and place." And that time and place, of course, is in response to God's orchestration behind the scenes. He brings people across my path, opens doors, whispers in my head, and waits for me to lean in. Then I get to do what He has gifted me to do. This was true freedom for me. I am called to be a supporter, an encourager, and a funder in partnership with other stewards actively involved in their expertise. So I am involved with mission work, a movie-making company, a honey business, a jewelry business, and several medical businesses—all while having no expertise in any of them. I simply apply my giftedness to help them.

NOT JUST A SIDE HUSTLE

My secular job and my ministry are not two ships passing in the night. God uses all things for His kingdom, including my "secular" job. I found it most efficient and effective for me to be self-funded, using my ability to generate income for the efforts I've felt God calling me to pursue. This is nothing new. It is the same tent-making approach the apostle Paul used. Not wanting to be a burden to anyone, he worked his way across the civilized world by sharing the gospel and making tents.

---

5   Walter Isaacson, *Steve Jobs* (New York: Simon & Schuster, 2011), 227.

By being self-funded, I do not take money out of the kingdom by asking others to support me. I put money into the kingdom through my business efforts. I am not suggesting that this is the only valid approach, only that it has been *my* calling because God has gifted me with profitable business expertise and resources.

I've had several people come to me seeking support. They usually say something like, "I feel called to be in ministry, so I'm going to raise support to pursue my calling."

What is the calling? Has it been identified? How have they distinguished themselves already as helpers of people wherever they have been? I understand the appeal of ministry, but when I'm not aware of what contribution they will make beyond a somewhat romanticized idea of "helping people," I can't help wondering who will fund all these idealistic missionaries. And to what end?

Am I suggesting that they should all be self-funded? Perhaps not. But when I think of John Enright's comment about the ineffectiveness of many missionaries he has seen in Africa, I think there should be some link between an aspiring missionary and an already existing pattern of effective ministry—at least ministry on a personal, relational basis with friends and relatives who need the Lord. If the beginning of the root system is there, I'm interested. If not, perhaps self-funding is a better approach.

CALLED TO BE A QUARTERMASTER

I liken my work in God's kingdom as that of a quartermaster. When my two sons entered scouting, I followed as an adult volunteer. I quickly learned about leadership principles taught through scouting ideals that have been handed down for over a century. They give young men (and old men like me) an opportunity to exercise leadership skills.

My involvement taught me the importance of mobilizing resources to take care of the boys while they enjoyed their scouting experience. The chief mobilizer was the quartermaster, and I learned the value of this position when I attended scoutmaster training. When I later became the head quartermaster of a scoutmaster training program, my duties included providing food, equipment, and resources to over one hundred fifty participants during the course. The many challenges gave me a deep appreciation for the diligence required in a quartermaster.

I know God has touched my heart to become a quartermaster for His kingdom, and I have learned to apply my scouting skills there. This includes not only resourcing the kingdom through donations but also stewarding all the resources entrusted to me. This requires creative problem-solving. It also requires that I maintain enough margin in life to respond when called upon. Being a quartermaster for a ministry is not a role for everyone, but I never cease to be thankful that God has called me to it, gifted and equipped me for it, and provides great fulfillment in it. He is the master planner.

HOW WE MOW THE GRASS SHOWS OUR EXCELLENCE

How do you mow the grass at your home? If you are a homeowner, you will more than likely take pride in keeping a neatly mowed and trimmed yard. You will mow it regularly and be concerned about how it appears to others. If you live in an apartment, you don't worry about the grass because others will mow it. If you rent a home, you may not always get around to mowing until the neighbors complain. You may mow sporadically to keep the weeds down, but you are unlikely to spend extra effort or money to maintain the yard. At least I don't know many renters who take pride in keeping up the yard of their rented house.

A similar principle is evident in ministry, church, and business. If we own something, we take better care of it. It has always been important to me that every employee in our firm would feel a sense of ownership in their projects—and with the client. Helping a client that you "rent" will not motivate you to provide service to them as if they were your client and your responsibility.

When I was a young architect working for others, I pretended that the clients were my own personal clients and that someday I would be able to "steal" them from my employer. That was not a bad motivation. It kept me sharp. It kept me servicing the clients as though they were my own. I delivered quality service that was both professional and prompt.

I have always encouraged our employees to have that same attitude. Yes, they could eventually leave the firm and take the client with them, but if we are servicing our client as we should, the client would probably remain loyal to the firm even if they liked the young architect. Allowing the employee to have the freedom, margin, and encouragement to "own" their projects and clients makes them much better professionals.

The same idea can be applied to ministry. I have noticed many mowing the grass as though they rent. A familiar passage with the encouragement to work hard—as unto the Lord—is Colossians 3:23–24: "Whatever you do, work at it with all your heart, as working for the Lord, not for human masters, since you know that you will receive an inheritance from the Lord as a reward. It is the Lord Christ you are serving" (NIV).

Some don't work that way. Many work, but few have the passion of ownership. God, like any good employer, wants us to own the mission of advancing His kingdom, to work with the heart of an owner rather than a renter.

Chapter 7

DEVELOPING ECONOMIC ENGINES

It is my belief that early in their careers, young men and women should learn to develop economic engines to serve God's kingdom. What do I mean by an economic engine? It's managing your abilities, giftedness, and resources to become sustainable—not only financially but with leadership. Ideally, this involves working with others to produce assets that contribute not only to your own needs but also to the needs of others. It can be as simple as developing job skills in a career that enables you to be self-funded for whatever form of ministry God has gifted you.

An economic engine is much like a normal engine that produces power and energy to accomplish something useful. Engines propel vehicles of many kinds. They drive tools and machinery and even generate electricity or other forms of energy. Engines multiply human effort and help power business economies and even societies.

Economic engines are also necessary to accomplish God's purposes within His kingdom. As businesses, they generate profits to support employee families as well as others in need. In God's economy, economic engines eventually benefit the poor.

MY ARCHITECTURAL ENGINE

Marydel and I went to the 1976 Campus Crusade for Christ Christmas Conference as an engaged couple. We were encouraged to "go on staff," as it was called in those days, to maximize our Christian potential in the world. We went through the interview process and were accepted to go to staff training the summer after we were married. The expectation was that we would go all in with our faith, becoming full-time staff members of what is now called Cru. Other staff members assured us that sharing Christ with students on campuses was the highest and best calling of our lives.

But our hearts were not in it. I still had the desire to be a business professional practicing architecture. We agonized over the decision, finally choosing to stay at the University of Oklahoma, where I would complete my master of architecture degree while Marydel worked as a part-time secretary and later as a teacher in a public high school.

Some of our friends made us feel like second-class Christians. From their perspective, we were not truly devoted to our faith. Otherwise, we would have prioritized ministry over secular careers. I kept looking in my rearview mirror, wondering if I had made the wrong turn by not going into ministry. But God assured me that I was on the right street even though I didn't fully understand it at the time.

I graduated and went to work for an outstanding architectural firm in Dallas, Texas. I worked for this well-known design firm for a year and then moved to another nationally recognized firm where I received equally good experience. I moved a third time to yet another excellent firm doing significant work all around Texas. All three of these firms gave me valuable professional work experience.

As a young architect, I had the desire to be a partner in one of these firms, but the opportunity never came. Subsequently, at the age of twenty-seven, I established my own firm. I had no idea at the time, but God was grooming me to develop an economic engine for His kingdom. I worked very hard during our first ten years as a small firm. We did excellent work and developed strong relationships in our commitment to provide the highest-quality professional service to our corporate clients.

It had never occurred to me that God had gifted me with the ability to generate income. This income included profit. And these profits began to accumulate. As we worked faithfully to serve our clients, we were given more work. As more work came in, we hired additional people and subsequently built a very large architectural firm. As one of the most prolific American architects, we provided architectural services to corporate clients in all fifty states. We worked for the world's largest architectural client for over thirty-five years: Walmart. We designed new stores, remodeled old ones, and added on to most of the remaining ones. Although we did not design all the stores, we provided architectural services for over eight thousand projects during these years. This enabled us to contribute to the massive good Walmart has provided our American culture: low prices for everyone, including the marginalized, while providing wonderful employment for millions as America's largest private employer.

By the end of my architectural career, our firm had completed over eight thousand projects. I venture to say that nearly everyone I have ever met has physically been in a building that our firm had either designed or remodeled over those years.

I personally did not take all the profit out of the firm. I shared a third of the profit with partners and a third with employees. The profits I retained have been—and are being—invested in God's kingdom. The amount of profit we accumulated is mind-boggling, especially since most architectural firms are not very profitable. Most firms fail within the first five years; very few ever reach their twenty-fifth anniversary. Our firm was thirty-seven years old when I sold it to younger partners and retired. During my tenure, we had a gross income that exceeded $500 million. We were selected as the number two corporate retail architectural firm in the country for three years in a row, and we were in the top five firms for five consecutive years.

I don't cite these facts to boast. I had very little to do with building this economic engine other than being faithful to the task God gave me. I firmly believe God gives people their opportunities, and He brought the income and wealth to our firm just as He gives all men and women their wealth. There is no way my talent could develop a firm this profitable without His blessing and opening doors for which I cannot take credit. I was faithful, God was even more faithful, and He had a plan for this economic engine to be used within His kingdom for His purposes.

One of the things I am most grateful for is that our economic engine generated profits that we invested in other economic engines. But I can't even take credit for that. I didn't know where to invest the money. I had to listen the best I could to discern the whispers of the Holy Spirit. Some of the efforts Marydel and I have invested in make no earthly sense. But they make a lot of sense in the bigger picture.

I do not believe in the prosperity gospel that says if we give to God, He'll give back more. This can easily lead to a give-to-get mentality that God can see right through. He knows our hearts, what motivates us, and how we will respond to the temptations of wealth, fame, or power. What I realized is that God gives generously to those whom He desires. It is not necessarily based on anything other than His almighty goodness and unsearchable wisdom. I realized that He had given me wealth and opportunity, and that I would stand before Him one day to give an accounting of it. Marydel and I live in holy fear of this accounting. It, however, gives us great joy to work in His kingdom when we know that we are being faithful.

Let me share some of the economic engines Marydel and I have empowered and supported along with several of our failures.

A BARBER FUNDING EVANGELISTS

One of the best economic engines I've ever seen is being built by a dear friend who happens to be my barber. I met Mulugeta over ten years ago when I sat in his barber chair for the first time at Shear Cuts.

I noticed a small Bible verse under the mirror on the wall in front of me. Nothing big, flashy, offensive, or glaring—simply a Bible verse. As he started cutting, I watched him in the mirror and said, "I see the verse you have under the mirror there. What's your story?"

"I am a Christian from Ethiopia. I emigrated from there several years ago."

"Fascinating," I said. "Tell me more. What was it like?"

"Well, I grew up in the countryside a long way from any city. My family was like most other families in the area, living in huts without electricity or running water. I wanted something more, so as a very young man I made my way to the capital city of Addis Ababa. I was able to get a job, but it didn't pay much. I lived inside a church in return for doing odd jobs for them. This helped me save some money so I could get an education. I was used to doing without much, especially before I got married." He flashed a smile.

"So you're married," I said. "Tell me about that."

"I met a beautiful young lady who was willing to marry me. Her name is Azeb. We had what you call the American dream. With problems in our country at the time, we wanted to immigrate to America. But that didn't mean we could. No one could emigrate without government approval. They controlled it very tightly with a lottery system. Only a few lucky ones could go. So we both applied. Azeb won. Dallas became our new home.

We had very little, but we were grateful to be here. One of the first things we did was to find some other Ethiopians and begin attending church with them. I went to cosmetology school and became a barber. I worked long hours to be able to afford a small apartment and take care of my family. Ethiopian babies eat a lot." There was that smile again.

As we talked, it became apparent that Mulu had a burden to go back to Ethiopia to share the good news of the gospel with his family and with others from his village. He even wanted to branch out beyond that to the surrounding mountainous countryside, most of which was Ethiopian Orthodox and hostile to Christianity.

After many haircuts with Mulu, a friendship developed. Eventually, the Holy Spirit nudged me, giving me the desire to help him return to Ethiopia for a visit. One evening, Marydel and I drove over to his apartment and sat down with his family. We handed him a check, and he began to cry.

Before long, the trip was set. Mulu took off to Ethiopia for three weeks. A friend picked him up in Addis Ababa and took him as close to his old home as he could get. From there, Mulu rode horseback up into the mountains, finally reaching the village where he had grown up. He found his elderly mother, a sister, and other relatives and enjoyed a wonderful visit with them.

God led Mulu to other men with whom he could partner to share the gospel with neighboring mountain folks. Most in that area are illiterate or did not have a written Bible. Knowing that, Mulu had taken solar-powered Proclaimer audio players and small MP3 players with the Bible in their native language so he could share the truth with them even after leaving.

Mulu traveled with these men for three weeks, sharing the gospel with all who would listen and leaving the players with groups that would meet to hear the Bible in their own language. Upon returning to the States, he employed three of these men to continue sharing the gospel throughout the countryside and mountain villages. Mulu supported each of these evangelists for the next few years at $150 per month, a good Ethiopian salary, that he paid from his own barber's salary. This was the start of Mulu's own personal ministry of utilizing local Christian workers to share the gospel for many years.

Fast-forward five years. Mulu was still working for Shear Cuts as a barber. He now had the desire to start his own barbershop. *Economic engine*, I thought. *Great, let's go for it!* Marydel agreed.

I wanted to help him buy a barbershop, but Marydel encouraged me to not be a part of the purchase. "I think you can help in other ways," she counseled, "but if you buy a place, it will take away a sense of ownership. Mulu is thrifty. Let's see what he can do."

She was right. He already had savings to make the purchase. We got to participate by helping remodel and update the space he had been able to buy. And now Mulu owns his own barbershop, purchased with his own money.

It's an awesome story, but it's far from over. Mulu and Azeb have four children. As I got to know him better, I realized what outstanding parents they were to their children. All four children seemed to be walking closely with the Lord. I watched how they were obedient to their parents, kindhearted, and certainly very polite to me. I knew that Mulu was dedicated to raising his family in a good, healthy Christian environment.

"The usual trim," I said as I slid into the chair one afternoon. "And I want to hear the latest on your kids."

"I am so proud of them," Mulu said. "My oldest daughter, you know she got a scholarship to college, right? Premed, and now she even got a scholarship to medical school! Who would have believed it? And my daughter will be a doctor? God is so good!"

"How about the younger ones?" I said, returning Mulu's grin.

"My second daughter is also in university. She's doing great too. Studying hard to get her physician's assistant degree. And the younger two, they're on the same path as their older sisters."

Mulu's family is an economic engine. They will be providing wonderful Christian workers in the medical profession for the next forty to fifty years. And who knows what God will call them to do? They've grown up seeing the example of parents who are totally committed to making a difference in the kingdom. They know it's not just talk or a faith of convenience. They, like many children, are very likely to replicate what they have seen firsthand and know is real.

It didn't take millions of dollars to affect the countryside of Ethiopia. It took just one faithful, hardworking man to build his small but powerful economic engine that would impact hundreds of people in the rural mountains of Ethiopia. On a barber's salary! He was faithful to save money to buy a barbershop, take care of his family, and raise godly children while faithfully stewarding resources to build God's kingdom. What an economic engine!

FAMILY AS AN ECONOMIC ENGINE

Marydel's and my investment in our own family is the most significant engine we built. We knew that we needed to raise our children to be devoted Christians and to be wise stewards of every resource entrusted to them.

Each of our children was allowed to manage money in college. We paid their tuition and gave them a housing allowance, but it was up to them to use it wisely. They needed to support themselves during every summer break by getting jobs, finding housing, and taking care of themselves. During their senior year, they received a housing allowance until April. After that, they needed to find permanent employment for their support.

We realized we were teaching our children to be resourceful and to be good stewards of their money. They have grown into fine adults with gainful employment, supporting children of their own.

Our children became economic engines because they generated income that they were able to share with others, especially those in need. We are so proud of them, not only because of their financial discipline but also because of their godly stewardship. One daughter and her husband supported Pine Cove's Camp in the City and helped establish an urban weeklong camp for marginalized children in their own local community. Our other children support many wonderful ministries and projects for God's kingdom. They support everything from investing in start-up businesses to providing significant support for nonprofits and Christian ministries. All our children are generous in giving to others.

As parents, our most important duty is to develop our children into faithful and good stewards and, hopefully, economic engines for the kingdom.

WHO DOESN'T LIKE A GOOD MOVIE?

In 2007, I met Jon and Andy Erwin, who had been hired by Crown Financial Ministries to produce videos for the ministry. I noticed that the Erwin brothers were exceptionally hardworking, extremely talented, and very young. Only in their twenties, they produced high-quality videos on a very limited budget. I realized they were exceptional, but I never thought I would get to work with them again.

Three years later, Jon and Andy had the idea of making a feature film. They simply needed the capital to bring their vision to life. So, with their parents and a family friend, we capitalized the Erwin Brothers with their first movie, *October Baby*. It was a small movie with a small release, only costing $800,000 to produce. But with their hard work and tremendous talent, the movie made the theaters in a small release by Sony Pictures. This movie hit the front page of the *New York Times* on April 4, 2012. Although the movie grossed only $5.3 million in theaters, Sony saw it as a great small picture that pointed to the Erwin brothers' potential, so the company decided to fund the next movie, *Moms' Night Out*.

What was once a small production company soon became Erwin Brothers Entertainment, and I joined them as founding partner. No, I'm not in the movie business. I just simply invest in two young men who are. But through Marydel and my initial capitalization, Erwin Brothers Entertainment has now produced ten movies with total box office receipts of over $200 million.

Erwin Brothers Entertainment provides what many would call faith-based movies. I don't like that term. We hope to produce really good movies that present God's kingdom to the general cinema audience. They are wholesome, and they show redemption, forgiveness, and reconciliation, and every thirteen-year-old girl or boy can watch any of them. The Erwin brothers are now known as outstanding talent in the industry. They've been given a wonderful opportunity to produce movies for years to come.

What started with a relatively small capitalization has grown into an economic engine as a serious entertainment company worth millions. What a fun and entertaining economic engine!

BUILDING AFRICAN BUSINESSES AS ECONOMIC ENGINES

As mentioned in the opening chapter, I traveled to Africa in 2008 with a group of businessmen to look for ways to help Crown Financial Ministries in Africa become financially sustainable. As we toured South Africa and several neighboring countries, we looked for opportunities to partner with existing efforts and develop new businesses to help fund the ministry. We took a side trip to Zambia, several countries north, where I originally met with John Enright, an entrepreneur, ministry leader, and long-time pastor.

John Enright grew up as a missionary kid in Congo and lived there much of his early life. With the civil unrest and atrocities in Congo, the family fled to Zambia. Having fled so quickly to a new country, John knew it would be almost impossible to continue the pastor-training school they had started if they couldn't develop additional financial resources. Rather than return constantly to the United States to fundraise, John dreamed of developing businesses to provide for this ministry. Although he used US donations to start, he later developed businesses in Zambia. Of the eleven businesses John started, nine failed to produce the profits needed for reliable income. Although they were good businesses and employed people, they couldn't cover the cost of the pastor-training school or the ministry needs. Two businesses finally worked and became the needed economic engines.

John was intelligent. Bordering on genius, he had a photographic memory. Everything he learned, he retained; what he retained, he applied. John would do research, think, and then ask God what he should do and how to apply what he had learned.

One example is when he applied research knowledge to build a honey company that started with a few beehives in the bush. More hives were built and the "ultimate" beehive was developed using the knowledge of an expert from Germany. It took numerous years, but after hard work, many failures, and a few successes, the ultimate beehive was deployed in the African bush. Sure enough, the bees came. And came. And kept coming. Soon John realized that more hives could be built and more people could be employed in the honey business. Fast-forward to the end of this story, and you will see the largest honey company in central Africa, now employing nine thousand village families. An astonishing 150,000 beehives were built and hang in trees all over central Zambia, Congo, and Tanzania.

Since the honey business flourished, John decided to look into developing another business. He realized that one goat, when it mated, could produce an average of 1.5 goats per year. If things went well, you would have a 100 to 150 percent increase each year. He also learned that mating large Boer goats imported from South Africa with the local village goats would be very economical. The hybrid goat was good for meat and was easily marketed and sold, both locally and overseas. Off to the goat races!

John surmised that the same villagers taking good care of his honey might also do well with the goats. His strategy was to build a goat house, give them twenty-five goats to start, and then come back and harvest the young goats for market. John generously shared the profits with the villagers, who did not make any financial investment. A pretty good deal for both.

Then John was tragically killed in a horrific car accident. I thought everything would come to a screeching halt. Thank God, I was wrong; He had other plans. John's faithful son and brother-in-law continued the businesses. They thrived—even without John's involvement—because of the hard work of their American partner, Chris Fread. Now, almost five years later, the honey business is booming. In a recent six-month period, they harvested over five hundred metric tons of honey. And the goat business is profitable as well with 120 operational goat farms.

These economic engines were started, and in part sustained, with capital that Marydel and I invested. We weren't the only funders, but we were involved very early to help John get started. The engines not only supplied the needs of thousands of villagers in central Africa but also provided funding to train pastors who would return to their communities to share the gospel. Retained earnings were sufficient to continue to expand the businesses and pay the salaries of those managing them.

Africa is definitely one of the hardest places to do business. Yet with determination, hard work, and ingenuity, these businesses have proven that the concept can work even there.

A JEWELRY COMPANY

Before I officially met Jenny McGee, I was sitting in a business seminar in Asia in 2010. Jenny's coworker sat down next to me and asked if she could share a unique business that Jenny had founded. As I listened, I was fascinated to learn of a jewelry company that Jenny had started to help women who had been exploited in the sex industry. I learned how they made and profitably sold jewelry while employing women from local brothels. Two days later, I met Jenny McGee, an American who had gone to Asia with her husband in 2006.

As Jenny walked the streets, she prayed for opportunities to share the love of Jesus. While walking by massage parlors and brothels, she noticed women who really pulled on her heart. She often thought to herself, *What can I do to help them?* Sometimes she would go in with the hope of becoming their friend. Being a creative, she thought, *Can we do something about this? Maybe we can make jewelry with their help.*

Fast-forward fifteen years. Jenny's Starfish Project is a high-quality boutique jewelry business producing the top sellers for the world's largest fair-trade accessories brands. Jenny's Starfish Project jewelry is sold by Kohl's and even sold fifty thousand units on *The Ellen DeGeneres Show*. Starfish Project also makes jewelry for other companies under their own brand names.

Jenny has now employed over two hundred women who have come out of sexual trafficking and exploitation. But far beyond just getting a job, these precious women now have hope, housing, support, and help taking care of their medical and emotional needs. By building this friendship community, survivors can work together, sort out their lives, and become truly successful.

To further their training, Jenny offers them the opportunity not only to make jewelry but also to learn Microsoft software and become skilled in computer applications useful in the mainstream office workforce. Many of the women become photographers, marketing experts, copywriters, and more, first for Starfish Project but then for other companies as well. And many, after they have healed, go on to marry and have children of their own. What a phenomenal success story! Ironically, Jenny also built friendships with several madams in the brothels, bringing them out to work at Starfish Project.

While many other nonprofit organizations were struggling to survive in Asia, Jenny built an economic engine to take care of these women while sharing the love of Jesus. And she didn't just proclaim this love. She also shared it through friendship, employment, and caring action. Her ministry became sustainable when she developed a legitimate, profitable business that affected several levels of society, penetrating the business market, the employment market, and even the brothels.

Starfish Project is one of the best economic engines I've ever seen. When I first met Jenny, I asked her what she needed. She told me that she needed capital so that Starfish Project could become a local corporation doing business in Asia. Marydel and I capitalized it at the outset and have since recapitalized it.

Jenny and I are partners in Starfish Project and in the kingdom. No, Marydel and I don't own any stock in Starfish Project, but we own a wonderful relationship that is dear to us and dear to many exploited women experiencing freedom in Asia.

MEDICAL CLINICS IN CENTRAL AFRICA

A mutual friend introduced me to Michael Spraggins in 2009. He told me that Michael was a businessman in Orlando, Florida, and wanted to make a midcourse correction in his business career. In the middle of building his construction materials company, he also wanted to make an impact for God's kingdom. He thought to himself, *What is the biggest problem in the hardest location?* He selected health care in one of the smallest and poorest countries in Africa and, for that matter, in the world. He thought to himself, *What can I do to help those in Burundi?* They have the poorest health-care system and the highest rates of child mortality.

He decided to provide good, clean medical drugs for the country. He began providing pharmaceuticals to be distributed by a faithful nursing staff. When I met him, the concept was new and unproven; it felt to me like the Wild West. I had no idea where it would go, but I felt prompted by the Holy Spirit to help him. Marydel and I gave what we call a "Kingdom Unit," $150,000 to assist his efforts. He was a new friend, and we were his first donor—in an unknown area and with an unproven concept. Not our norm, for sure, but Michael was an extremely hardworking, smart CPA who knew how to pursue his dream with diligence. Cue the starting gun.

The reality of distributing drugs through a nursing staff wasn't viable. The desire to help the Burundian population with medical care soon evolved into a church-based health clinic idea called LifeNet. Michael was smart enough to get help from medical experts. These included the top nursing educator from Israel, along with others from the US, to develop a program and educate local medical staff. At the time, Burundi had only three hundred medical doctors in the whole country, and most of them had been trained in-country at a standard below most of the world. Nevertheless, he had to begin with what was there, not what he would have liked. Success had to come by working within the existing system to establish three foundational components.

First was remedial medical training. LifeNet began training nursing staff and others to provide higher-quality medical services. Most had received little if any medical training, and many had the equivalent of only a ninth-grade level of education.

Second was medical equipment. Michael noticed that most clinics had very little equipment and couldn't afford to buy any. He determined to provide loans to buy microscopes, resuscitation devices, and simple testing equipment. Nothing exotic or complicated, just basic equipment for lifesaving procedures.

Third was business training. LifeNet provided this training along with business loans to launch the beginning of what would become complete health care.

Prior to Michael's vision for LifeNet, 12 percent of babies died at birth, sometimes joined by their mothers. Through Michael's leadership and vision, the LifeNet staff grew and trained others, who trained others, who trained still others. Utilizing this "train the trainer" model, the LifeNet staff trained literally thousands of medical personnel in Burundi, Uganda, and Congo, upgrading the medical profession significantly.

LifeNet expanded into adjacent countries, providing high-quality health care to existing systems. The same three foundational elements—upgraded medical training, financial resources to buy necessary equipment, and business training to become sustainable—were introduced. LifeNet put the whole package together while saving multitudes of precious lives. As of 2022, LifeNet has conducted over twenty-seven million patient visits in 383 medical clinics in Burundi, Uganda, Malawi, Kenya, Ghana, and Congo. As a result of LifeNet's efforts, over 160,000 babies were safely delivered, and 3,984 babies and their mothers were saved in 2022.[6]

6   LifeNet International, *2022 Annual Report*, April 21, 2021, https://www.lninternational.org/wp-content/uploads/2022/12/LifeNet-2022-Annual-Report.pdf.

LifeNet charges for its services, but its income is not able to cover all costs. Financial help from US individuals and foundation grants currently augment the sustainable model that is continuing to grow. It is an engine in central Africa to provide high-quality medical care, bringing God's kingdom to the poor in one of the hardest places.

AN ECONOMIC ENGINE FOR DAY CAMPING

During the 2007–2008 economic recession, Christian camps throughout America suffered. Pine Cove Camp in Tyler, Texas, was no exception. Its CEO, Mario Zandstra, came up with a terrific idea, not realizing at the time that he was creating an economic engine.

Pine Cove normally housed a total of twenty thousand campers each summer in weeklong camp sessions. It was quite expensive to go to Pine Cove, and only middle- and high-income families could send their children. Many lower-income and inner-city kids would never have the chance to experience a residential camp like this.

Mario's brainstorm was to flip the flow. If the children could not come to the camp, he would take the camp to the children, going to the cities with staff and equipment and allowing churches to host Pine Cove on their own turf. He calculated that $150,000 for equipment to set up the mobile experience, including recruiting the staff, would meet the need.

Campers could come all week during the day from 9 a.m. to 4 p.m. and enjoy the great Pine Cove experience without needing to spend the night. Camp in the City gave them outstanding biblical teaching in a camplike setting. College students hired for the summer got the blessing of being counselors. The church ministered by using its facilities to host the camp and by providing housing with church families for the counselors. For many of the kids who attended, it was a new experience: not just getting to go to a camp but even setting foot in a church. This gave the church an opportunity to bless these children along with their own church members.

Camp in the City was self-sustainable because the lower cost to operate made it affordable for the campers' families. Enough margin was generated each summer to launch Camp in the City for the following summer.

WHY INVEST IN A BODY REPAIR SHOP?

My son developed some very close friendships during his college years. Preston was one who became dear to our family as he spent time with our son and visited our vacation home in Wyoming. As I got to know Preston, I noticed he was very sharp and witty and had a great work ethic. After having worked in the consulting business for numerous years, he decided to buy a business and develop his own economic engine. Marydel and I assisted with a simple loan to help purchase a body repair shop.

Why would a business consultant buy such a business? Preston had several things in mind. First, he wanted to buy a small business that he could turn around and make profitable. Second, he wanted to employ people he could minister to by being a good employer. Many minorities work in this industry, and he felt that if he could buy this business and make it more profitable, he could employ more people in need of a good, steady job. Finally, since excellence is a requirement for business success, he determined to provide the highest-quality body work possible by making sure his employees enjoyed and took pride in their work. This economic engine met the needs of not only Preston's family but also the many families working for him in the business.

A PONZI SCHEME

Not everything that Marydel and I have invested in has worked. One of the economic engines we tried to build involved a young African leader from Rwanda.

I spent several years with this young man, meeting with him consistently and mentoring him—or so I thought. He was part of the business office staff in the executive suite of a large church we attended. He was also a scamster.

This young man asked us to invest in him as he developed much-needed technical resources for those doing business in Africa. I thought we were investing in a system that would allow Africans to conduct business simply on their phone. "Business in a Box" included ways to transact financial business by having accounting functions, inventory functions, credit card usage—all within an app on the phone. It all looked legitimate, and development seemed to be ongoing. But it was simply a Ponzi scheme. He collected money from early investors, showed false results, and paid back his early investors with new investor money, defrauding the later ones.

It finally blew apart two years into its operation. Just as Paul says in 1 Corinthians 4:5, "[the Lord] will bring to light what is hidden in darkness and will expose the motives of the heart" (NIV). Once he was exposed, several investors and I pursued him with an attorney to try to recover some of our investment. He fled the country, leaving his wife and children. What looked good on the outside deceived many smart people. And this is one time I got totally blindsided.

AN APP THAT SHOULD HAVE WORKED BUT DIDN'T

Another venture that failed to be financially profitable was still great for God's kingdom. A friend of mine decided to develop an app to encourage people to get into Bible study, meditation, and journal writing. This was in the early days of apps, when they were just starting on iPhones and Androids. A lot of work went into it, and it looked excellent. We expected to fund the business through advertising revenues. The app worked as intended, and people used it. Unfortunately, we couldn't find the advertising revenue necessary to keep it operational, let alone pay back the original investment. After several years, the app was officially shut down.

I know my investment did a lot of good, especially for me because it was a dip into the tech business—something I needed to learn about although it didn't bring a financial return.

TURBO ENGINES

I've noticed that God has entrusted large resources to certain stewards to be deployed in His kingdom through humility and obedience. In the examples that follow, the engines began as relatively small efforts. God gave their builders the ability to create wealth, and they were obedient to serve Him with it. These engines now affect a great part of the world through their financial turbo power.

Barnhart Crane & Rigging evolved from a small towing business to one of the largest in the industry of lifting and moving huge and heavy items. As the second generation of owners, the Barnhart brothers decided to dedicate their business to the glory of God and to use the profits to further His kingdom. Through the extreme generosity of these two brothers and their wives, many organizations have been funded to do great things.

In the 1970s, David and Barbara Green started a small craft business. God caused their business, Hobby Lobby, to grow into a large national retail concern. Their son Mart Green later started Mardel, what has now become a national chain of bookstores. The Green family dedicates 50 percent of their retail business profits to support many ministry organizations. Chief among their efforts have been the creation of the Museum of the Bible in Washington, DC, and Bible translation efforts throughout the world.

David Weekly founded what is now the largest privately owned home-building company in America. Realizing that God created him for stewardship, he allocates 50 percent of his time and income to nonprofits. Much of his focus supports the work of social entrepreneurs building innovative organizations to serve the world's poorest people.

As men and women eagerly help others and provide excellent service, their businesses become turbo engines for change. Walmart has been a tremendous economic benefit to almost everyone through their low prices and philanthropy in their local communities. Southwest Airlines, as the largest domestic carrier, has provided excellent service to their customers for well over forty years. Servant-hearted leadership and generosity to their communities and customers have been their hallmark. Interstate Battery, through its founder Norm Miller, has empowered literally thousands of other men and women to have their own businesses and to fund numerous causes for God's kingdom. My dear friend John Enright built one of the largest African companies through his honey business to service the poor.

These businesses are turbo engines used by God in His kingdom. Never underestimate the power of small beginnings and faithful obedience. The benefits to humankind are enormous through the efforts of these founders and subsequent servant leaders as they further God's kingdom by caring for those around them. These supercharged engines are indicative of men and women who have committed their God-given assets to build His kingdom as fast as they can. They know their wealth doesn't make them any holier than other good stewards who have different God-given resources, talents, or opportunities.

They just operate on a different scale but with the same goal of glorifying God.

Economic engines can be big and grandiose, and they can be as small as a barbershop or body repair shop. They can work at all scales and in most locations and industries. The important thing is that they implement biblical business principles to build God's kingdom on earth.

Chapter 8

THE CHIEF PURPOSE OF BUSINESS
IN GOD'S ECONOMY

There I was, stomach satisfied by a delightful breakfast, sitting in my well-appointed office, and reading with my feet up on the desk. I looked almost like the businessman caricature except without the cigar or brandy. All in all, I was feeling pretty good as I started reading a newsletter from a small ministry in Lesotho, Africa.

Then it hit me, the quote from Richard Stearns, former president of World Vision.

> For I was hungry, while you had all you needed. I was thirsty, but you drank bottled water. I was a stranger, and you wanted me deported. I needed clothes, but you needed *more* clothes. I was sick, and you pointed out the behaviors that led to my sickness. I was in prison, and you said I was getting what I deserved.[7]

---

7   Richard Stearns, *The Hole in Our Gospel* (Nashville, TN: Thomas Nelson, 2009), 59.

My heart broke. What was I doing to minister to the people on God's heart? In that moment I felt convicted about simply being where I was—living in an affluent country, sitting in my luxurious office with my feet on the desk. But such convictions are sometimes no more than diversionary tactics from the Enemy; my location wasn't the issue. The real questions remained: What am I doing to minister to the people on God's heart? What is my responsibility and the purpose of my business? Greater yet, what is the chief purpose of all business in God's kingdom? I began to wonder, *Is the chief purpose of kingdom business to be an economic engine to take care of the poor?*

BUSINESSPEOPLE AS STEWARDS

It's a logical assumption that God will use businesspeople to perform a unique stewardship role. No one is better qualified in God's kingdom to be stewards of resources than businesspeople. They have the ability to develop human capital, generate employment, and create wealth for economic expansion. Frontline workers, although very important to productivity, don't generally have the mindset or array of skills needed to advance economic development.

As I've contemplated why God gave me the ability to establish and maintain a large architectural firm, I am convinced that it is to glorify Him by being a steward to serve those on His heart. I also know that part of my stewardship role is to generate profit in my business, just as the faithful stewards in Jesus' parables did.

THE GOAL OF KINGDOM BUSINESS

The goal of any business is to generate profit to reward its investment risk and sustain itself. It does this by earning more revenue than it spends or consumes. This is true of kingdom business as well, but kingdom business has another layer of responsibility: to do what is right. This requires it to demonstrate righteousness and justice in how its profits are obtained because these qualities are at the heart of God's character.

What should stewards do with profits in order to receive the Lord's commendation? Several priorities exist. First, they should take care of their immediate family. Second, they should take care of their employee family, enabling employees to support their families through fair wages and, when possible, even sharing in the company's profit. A generous work environment helps sustain financially healthy employees who help sustain the business itself.

However, if all profit were spent on excessive overhead and employee bonuses, nothing would be left to maintain and expand the economic engine generating those profits. Prudent reinvestment in the company is crucial for the healthy continuance of the economic business engine.

Once these priority uses of profit are met, where else should profits be deployed? Many business owners use the remaining profits for their own exclusive consumption (or hoarding). But business owners who are stewards in God's kingdom know a higher purpose: storing treasures (investments) in heaven. They have clear vision to see through the foolishness of the rich farmer from Luke 12, whom we looked at in chapter 5. When this farmer had surplus, he hoarded it to maintain his lifestyle of ease. But this is what happened:

> God said to him, "You fool! This very night your life will be demanded from you. Then who will get what you have prepared for yourself?"
>
> This is how it will be with whoever stores up things for themselves but is not rich toward God. (Luke 12:20–21 NIV)

A consistent theme from Genesis through Revelation is God's requirement for His people to care for those in need, including the poor who are unable to take care of themselves.

This is the essence of kingdom investment. Jesus described "the least of these my brothers" (Matthew 25:40) as the hungry, thirsty, unclothed, foreigner, alien, and the prisoner (vv. 35–36). It is no stretch to include the abused, exploited, enslaved, abandoned and unrepresented in their number as "religion that God our Father accepts as pure and faultless is this: to look after orphans and widows in their distress" (James 1:27 NIV).

HELPING THE POOR

According to Proverbs 19:17, when we are generous to the poor, we lend to the Lord, and He will repay us. I think being repaid by God is likely to be the best possible return on investment. If business profits in the kingdom economy are to funnel down to help those in need, the provision must be done in a healthy, dignified, and compassionate manner without harm to recipients. I have seen the good intentions of relief undermine local economies in third-world countries. Helping the poor should not simply be a financial transaction. It should also be done in a relationship with those being served. This is the only way to determine when it is a hand up rather than merely a handout.

It may seem efficient to distribute wealth to the poor all at once, but this risks two problems. First, it sets up an attitude of dependency because it doesn't allow the recipients of the money to learn money-building habits that will sustain them and their families for generations. Second, when funds are exhausted, the flow stops, potentially creating a worse condition than before the distribution began. Building an economic engine, however, enables people to do meaningful work with dignity that continues to generate profits and allow ongoing income.

Although it's a bold statement, I argue that the chief purpose of business in God's kingdom is to become an economic engine to funnel down profit to help those in need. In doing so, the business steward serves the Lord by taking care of "the least of these my brothers," to which the King will reply, "You did it to me" (Matthew 25:40).

GOD'S ECONOMIC DESIGN

God chooses stewards who realize that all wealth is given by Him to accomplish His kingdom purposes. God allows His stewards discretion in how they specifically apply His principles in enacting His economic design. And He provides guidance through His Spirit as stewards ask for it and become humble listeners. When affluent Christians do not depend on the Holy Spirit as they make decisions but simply ask God to bless whatever they choose, God may still use them in spite of the broken and messy lives that often result. The result may be better than nothing, but it's not what it could be.

In Psalm 72, Solomon asked God for two things, both of which impacted the economic design of his kingdom. He asked for wisdom to (1) righteously judge the people and (2) enact justice for the poor. He realized what a linchpin this was for the welfare of his entire kingdom—not just the poor.

The entrepreneur in God's kingdom should aspire to be like Solomon in this regard. The prerequisite for success is to fear, worship, and serve God, respecting His overall economic design. God's design for stewards is to be esteemed leaders, honored and entrusted to enact righteousness and justice for the greater community.

When righteousness prevails, so does good will. Prosperity naturally occurs when corruption and oppression are not tolerated. Under the rule of righteous law, industry springs up and gainful employment follows. People establish small businesses when fair payment for services is rendered. A healthy economy contributes to peace and growing freedom for those who have been marginalized and abandoned. All this comes as righteous men and women create and use profits to bless the needy around them.

RIGHTEOUSNESS AND JUSTICE

Righteousness and justice are the foundation of God's throne and form the backbone of a culture. Nations are built through the muscle of their labor force—most of which comes from the lower half of the socioeconomic bracket. How tragic and paralyzing it is, then, when many laborers in third-world countries have no opportunity to work. Poverty ravages a community absent of any reasonable hope of people working to support their families. But when righteous leaders step forward to provide opportunities for the poor to work, the whole economy begins to rise and flourish.

God's economic design is meant to protect the weak and vulnerable. When justice prevails, the marginalized and poor are protected from oppressors. Righteous leaders defend the afflicted by creating a system of laws that favor fairness and punish oppressors.

When a society fails to protect the poor and vulnerable, who takes up their cause? The poor can lose everything they have worked for if corruption and injustice go unchecked. What good is a microloan to a poor widow if her crops are stolen by bullies at harvest? How about the father who gets imprisoned for his inability to repay debt because of exorbitant or illegal interest rates? What about young girls kidnapped from their villages or lured to the cities by employment opportunities only to be enslaved in sex trafficking? Without leaders stepping forward, billions miss the opportunity to participate in God's economic design.

THE WORLD'S ECONOMY VERSUS GOD'S ECONOMY

The world's economy is motivated by selfishness—everyone for themselves. Those with less are oppressed and degraded; those with more are jealously criticized.

This is evidenced in the poorest of third-world countries. When traveling through sub-Saharan Africa, I am quite taken by the lack of infrastructure and development. Roads are unfinished, bridges never built, and utilities nonexistent. The wealthy drive Mercedes on rough dirt roads to their protected compounds.

Why is this normal? Leaders and their societies are disconnected. They don't understand the relationship between their circumstances and those of the neglected, abandoned, and poor people. Therefore, the economy that would naturally provide infrastructure, prosperity, and peace never seems to develop.

God's economy is just the opposite. It elevates the poor rather than tearing them down. That's what brings prosperity to a nation and society. Raising up "the least of these" enables a society to flourish and its leaders and stewards to be blessed.

Although prosperity is certainly not the cure for all the ills of fallen humankind, God has made it clear that He cares about the downtrodden, the hopeless, those so burdened by their effort to merely survive that they can't even begin to think about the purpose of life or fulfilling their potential.

Given an opportunity, many will work hard to learn and grow, to take care of their own families and those around them. A country has no greater capital than its human ingenuity and workforce. It's a beautiful design when righteous governance enables a society to flourish. And godly businesspeople are lights in darkness to help show the way.

Chapter 9

INVESTMENT OPPORTUNITIES

THE VEGETABLE GARDEN

Several years ago I started a very small urban vegetable garden at our home. In fact, it was so small that you might not have noticed it in my backyard unless I told you beforehand. Running alongside the back wall, it was only eighteen inches wide. But did that vegetable garden produce for us! I learned an interesting lesson about agricultural economics in the relationship between plant type and yield. There is also a relationship between cost of plants verses the value of produce during the life of the plant.

If I want my gardening to be sustainable, I need more produce coming off a plant than it cost to plant and grow it. I learned that lesson quickly when I planted broccoli and brussels sprouts. Initially, they sprang quickly into beautiful broad-leaved plants. In fact, they grew so big that they took over a large part of the garden area. Then at the top of the stem came the bloom. The broccoli produced a big clump of broccoli, and the brussels sprouts began to grow up the stalk. But what I realized is that the small plant that cost $2.69 would yield only about $1.69 worth of produce. Not only that, but each one took up an eighteen-by-eighteen-inch area, too large a space in such a small garden. And they began to crowd out adjacent peppers.

I also noticed the greediness of my squash plants. The huge leaves covered a big part of the remaining garden. They took up room, and most of the blossoms didn't produce fruit. Another fail.

What I found to be incredibly successful were pepper and tomato plants, which produced pounds of produce. In fact, the tomato plants grew four feet tall and yielded large quantities of cherry tomatoes or many huge, luscious tomatoes. The yields were so great that I had to prop the plants up with stakes to keep them from breaking. The pepper plants grew up to six feet tall, yielding incredible numbers of peppers. I had jalapeños as well as beautiful, sweet bell peppers. They continued producing for months, starting in early March, until a serious freeze in December. We had peppers, peppers, and more peppers.

And then there was the cantaloupe. One small plant yielded five large cantaloupes over the summer. Another phenomenal success and economic gain! My onions were underground, so I couldn't see them as well. But in the end, my experience was one onion down means one onion out—not much more. No hope for multiple onions.

Of course you know where I'm going with this: planting a vegetable garden is like investing in ministries. The comparisons are obvious. Some ministries yield one for one, like my onions. Others are more like my pepper plant with its incredible yield. It didn't take much to get it started, and once it started producing, it just multiplied.

HOW I INVEST IN GOD'S KINGDOM

I certainly can't tell others where to invest in God's kingdom, but I can give my experience. It's only when we stand before the Lord in the final accounting of our lives that we know how effective we've been in things that truly matter to Him. But let me share a few things I've found helpful.

First, I listen to the whispers of the Holy Spirit. He speaks quietly. Sometimes His voice seems like my conscience, sometimes a nudge that may be slight or strong, emotional or not. And sometimes it is difficult to distinguish from my own thoughts. You may remember that when I first met John Enright, I felt the Holy Spirit whispering for me to give him a large gift to help his sustainable ministry projects. Marydel and I work closely together to discern what the Holy Spirit seems to be telling both of us. Unity in our conviction regarding the Spirit's prompting is an important part of ensuring that we give the right amount at the right time.

Second, I invest deliberately. I intentionally set aside money to invest in future opportunities that I trust God to reveal when the time is right. This relieves pressure when requests are made of us. We are ready if the Lord confirms, but we are also convinced that obedience means saying no when we don't sense His confirmation. I know this can be difficult to define but let me assure you that it's not about investing emotionally or just when we get a feeling.

Marydel and I normally plan our annual giving and set our generosity goals. This provides a guideline and helps protect us from urgent appeals and emotional pressure that have nothing to do with the Spirit's prompting for us. Part of the equation is deliberately and regularly focusing on the things God has revealed to us as being important to Him and in alignment with our spiritual gifts and motivation.

Third, we take risks and have courage even when we don't see outcomes. There is a risk-reward balance in all investments, including those in God's kingdom. We don't expect high rewards for low risks, nor do we accept high risk for low rewards. The higher the risk, the closer an investment comes to gambling, and we don't see that as the mindset of a faithful steward. One protection is refusing to invest in things we don't understand.

On the other hand, we know that the commended stewards in the parable of the talents took risks that enabled them to double their master's money. We don't want to be so conservative that we try to remove all risk when investing in the kingdom. So we pray for wisdom and attempt to exercise it in understanding and obeying God's promptings.

I took a big risk on two young movie makers to make their first movie when they were in their twenties. It wasn't a blind risk because I knew who they were and had worked with them on other projects. But to make a feature-length movie was a big risk. After ten years in business with them, the risk has paid off with numerous successes and a couple failures. Overall, the risk has been well worth the effort and the financial return.

I've also taken significant risk when loaning money without collateral. There have been several instances where I have loaned money to individuals whom I knew well as an investment in their projects or businesses. Without collateral or any certainty of success, the money was clearly at risk. I've had several losses but have also been repaid by most. Although my potential gain is not nearly as great since loans are usually made at an established interest rate, it has certainly helped the borrowers build their businesses and, thus, the kingdom.

Let me add that I generally don't recommend lending money to friends. I'd much rather give them the money than require them to pay it back and risk straining the friendship. But in equity partnerships or other business arrangements where I invest money, I expect a return. I realize that I may never see the money again, but if I feel led to go ahead, it is because I judge the risk to be worth the potential impact in God's kingdom.

THREE PARTS OF AN INVESTMENT

The three main parts of any investment are (1) the amount invested, (2) the rate of return expected, and (3) the investment time period. Although all three parts are important, the amount invested and the rate of return are not as critical as the time period because a small amount invested at a modest rate over a long period of time will grow more than a large amount over a short period of time. These same factors also relate to investing in the kingdom of God through ministries and nonprofits.

When investing in the kingdom, the sooner money goes in, the longer it has to produce fruit. The longer it can be productive, the lower the dollar amount required to achieve an equivalent return. We never know how long investors will live and retain their ability to invest, but the sooner they make a particular investment, the greater the benefit even if the rate of return stays the same.

This influences me to invest as soon as possible in whatever effort I feel led by the Holy Spirit to support. And this is taking into account only the earthly perspective on kingdom investing, not the miraculous effects of God's blessing. If He is prompting me to participate in something He intends to accomplish, my anticipated rates of return will be dwarfed by what He does behind the scenes. Just as He has worked in my heart and mind to influence my obedience, He is at work in others.

The incredible rates of multiplication I've seen in my architectural firm—as well as the honey, movie, and jewelry businesses I've invested in—would never have happened without God's hand. In kingdom economics, efforts can return a thirty-, sixty-, or one-hundred-fold increase. God, the author of life, delights in multiplying life. Why delay investing?

SPIRITUAL AND SECULAR INVESTMENT WORLDS

I don't believe we should differentiate between the spiritual and the secular when it comes to working or investing in God's kingdom. God is Lord. He owns everything, and He has never abdicated His ownership. We own nothing in God's kingdom. We are simply managers and stewards of what He has entrusted to us. A business owner striving to be a good steward is on a sacred mission that is just as holy as a nonprofit ministry.

In explaining what I do and how we invest in God's kingdom, I use the illustration of mixing up my peas and carrots in mashed potatoes. As a little boy, I used to mix up my vegetables every time my mom served warm mashed potatoes. For me, nothing was more delightful than eating them all at once. I guess that's also why I so enjoyed chicken pot pie. So much of what I do combines for-profit business and nonprofit ministry, just like my mixed vegetables.

I don't think God's economy has different silos for businesses than for nonprofits. He calls His stewards in both to be accountable, making it equally holy to give money to charity or to build a business that becomes an economic engine for God's kingdom. God created both business and economies, and as we have seen, He even gives men and women their opportunities and wealth.

I can—and do—give to God's kingdom out of either checkbook, the one that gets a tax deduction for donations or the one that does not. For me, deductibility may be an incentive, but it never drives my decision to invest.

I especially enjoy working with men and women in organizations and businesses that generate profit for God's kingdom. More and more, I realize that the discipline of making a profit is actually helpful in running kingdom work because it enforces a diligence that otherwise can fade over time.

THERE HAS TO BE A BENEFIT

When asking someone to donate to an organization or a cause, a clear benefit must exist. By human nature and God's design, we all work for rewards and want to see accomplishment. There's nothing wrong with that; it's the way God made us. So when organizations, ministries, and nonprofits ask for money, the donor should also benefit.

Some organizations want money and maybe a relationship to sustain future funding. This seems so transactional. When I work with organizations or ministries, I want comradery and something in return for my investment. I don't want just a report or verbal justification. I want to have a sense that there is also a benefit to me for using hard-earned, saved money to help their cause or organization. This is not selfish; it's natural. We are fooling ourselves to think we do it "just because." Let me give you an example.

When I was vice president of the American Institute of Architects (AIA) in Dallas, Texas, I volunteered to help raise money for the new AIA offices. It wasn't our policy to borrow money for such projects, so fundraising was apparently the only available option. But most architects don't enjoy giving money just because they are "good people." Architecture is not a lucrative profession, and I find most architects to be frugal. To raise funds from architects in our professional society, I had to be creative and give them some benefit for their donations. I came up with the idea that there should be a benefit that was valuable to their firms but of little cost to the AIA.

I approached ten architectural firms and met with their managing partners individually. The executive director of the AIA and I took each of them to lunch and explained that we wanted them to follow my lead as the initial donor. Our firm put up $50,000 as seed capital for the $500,000 project. I simply asked the owners of each firm if they would match my donation.

In return they would get publicity, advertising, respect, and honor throughout the profession. The Dallas community at large would learn of their generous contribution, and the membership would see it displayed in a profile article honoring their firm. This advertising and prominence, although costing the AIA nothing, was valuable to the firms. Trying to get the publicity through a PR firm would be quite costly and possibly look like self-aggrandizement. But being honored and appreciated by the profession was a better way to bring them honor.

I had ten lunches and was able to raise $50,000 from each of the ten firms. Everyone seemed to be excited to be founding partners of the new Dallas Center for Architecture. The AIA gave these partners benefits such as exclusive use of the facility for functions and continuing education classes for their firms.

Organizations and nonprofits can creatively give benefits to donors without having to spend a lot of money. And in my opinion, the best way an organization can benefit a donor is by properly managing their donations to achieve their intended purpose. When stewards perform well and do what they promise, donors feel rewarded, respected, and honored.

My priority is not earthly rewards. I'm looking for future rewards as a good and faithful servant in God's kingdom. Some investments in God's kingdom yield a financial profit so money can be recycled again. That's good. And sometimes money should just be given to feed the poor. That's also good because God says it's like giving to Him.

GIVING JOYFULLY OR UNDER COMPULSION?

I strive to give joyfully and not under compulsion or pressure. "Each of you should give what you have decided in your heart to give, not reluctantly or under compulsion, for God loves a cheerful giver" (2 Corinthians 9:7 NIV). I usually don't like being asked for donations because it puts pressure on me. Sometimes the Holy Spirit gives me the desire to give (without being asked) to certain organizations, people, or projects as a steward and not just a reactive donor.

THE DANGERS OF PLEDGING

"Like clouds and wind without rain is a man who boasts of a gift he does not give" (Proverbs 25:14).

Promises made but not fulfilled can be a great discouragement, just like desperately needing rain in a drought. In a moment of excitement, I know one young man who committed to give 10 percent of his business profits to a certain cause. The business had tough times, and profits didn't materialize as anticipated. The commitment was forgotten.

I've also been guilty of making commitments that I later forgot. I hate to say it, but it has happened several times. As a result, I've experienced pain and regret—but probably not to the extent of those who were counting on me to fulfill the pledge. This verse from Proverbs has reminded me that oaths, commitments, and promises are vital to those relying on them. It's better not to make promises than to make them and not fulfill them.

SIMPLE INVESTMENTS WITHOUT A DEDUCTION

What are some simple and practical investments we can make in God's kingdom? Have you ever thought about those who serve us in the jobs we are unwilling to do ourselves? One of the practical things I can do is to tip well. When staying in a hotel, I tip the cleaner. Leaving money on the bathroom counter is an expression of appreciation and shows God's love for those who serve us. I have many times tipped the airport janitor who keeps the facilities tidy. A friend of mine "tithes" to valets who park his car. Many times, he'll give a valet attendant a twenty-dollar bill. Giving in this manner is giving when no one is looking; we don't receive credit or a contribution receipt, but we get an inner reward that is even more valuable—to say nothing of whatever eternal value may accrue.

Have you considered a gift to those who are on the street? Yes, there are those who simply need money to survive. Others are deceptive panhandlers. It's easy to make a quick judgment and say, "They'll just use what I give for liquor or other things I don't approve of." But what if you were that needy person? How would you want someone to respond? Well, if I were on the street, I would want a "fat cat" like me to give. I strive to not be self-righteous and determine their motivations at this point. Simply giving money mercifully to those who ask shows mercy to those who may desperately need it.

MENTORING THE NEXT GENERATION

As marketplace leaders, we have a great impact on the lives of young men and women coming behind us, the generations that will replace us. There are some things that only we can do. I often ask the Lord, *What am I gifted to do in this situation that no one else can do as well?* One of the answers is often investing in the younger generation through mentorship. When they look to older leaders for wisdom and counsel, I get a lot of bang for my buck. So I've decided to be available to them, to never deny access to the knowledge and experience God has led me to accumulate. I ask Him to bring those who are teachable.

Paul, in his many dialogues with Timothy, encouraged him to mentor others. Their relationship was deep, almost like a father and son. While Paul was imprisoned in Rome, he gave Timothy both encouragement and marching orders. Sensing that he was nearing the end of his life and that this could be their last communication, Paul wanted to ensure that Timothy was well supplied with knowledge and validation from his mentor. This stewardship of leadership rings clear in 2 Timothy 2:2: "What you have heard from me in the presence of many witnesses entrust to faithful men, who will be able to teach others also."

Paul had been entrusted with the gift of the gospel. He entrusted his knowledge and experience to Timothy, training him to be a coworker in spreading the beautiful news about Jesus. Then he completed the cycle by instructing Timothy to steward the gospel to additional faithful people.

In 2 Timothy 2:15–20, Paul told Timothy to be a worker who was not ashamed, rightly handling the word of truth, a vessel ready for every good work. This applies to us today. As men and women of great wealth and resources, we have the privileged opportunity of working in God's kingdom while on earth by mentoring the next generation of marketplace leaders.

Over the past thirty-five years, I have had the privilege of influencing two hundred of the three hundred fifty professionals in my architectural firm. Not everyone gets an allocation of time, but I have spent significant time with many of them, including three of my younger business partners.

Mentoring takes time, and sometimes that requires sacrifice. With numerous young men asking for such time, I endeavor to make time for those I sense are seeking wisdom. This happens in a variety of ways. I met with one at six o'clock in the morning to run at the lake. With many others I had monthly or quarterly lunches, and with several more, one-on-one Bible studies. I am confident that they will continue to grow in wisdom because of their diligent attitudes as well as their bright minds.

FINANCING THE NEXT GENERATION

I again ask myself, *What am I uniquely qualified to do?* Along with mentorship, I've realized that I am also suited to invest financially in young, hardworking, and talented leaders. I've invested in young men and women in their late twenties to midthirties to help them develop economic engines to work within God's kingdom. Some are artists, some are entrepreneurs, and some are just hardworking folks. This kind of investing usually results in a double bottom line: sure, it makes money, but it also provides social value by supporting employees.

When I'm looking for good investment partners, I look for diligent, talented young people. To me it doesn't matter whether we partner in a nonprofit, a ministry, or a for-profit business. Each of these is a long runway, and as with almost any start-up, you never know if it will succeed at the beginning. Giving mentorship, counsel, and capital greatly increases the odds of their takeoff to a successful flight.

As Paul was finishing his last letter to Timothy, he said affectionately, "Do your best to come to me soon" (2 Timothy 4:9). Shortly after, he added, "Bring the cloak that I left" (v. 13), and "Do your best to come before winter" (v. 21). This is the same kind of personal relationship and affection we should strive to have with those we mentor. Some day when I'm old, I hope one of these young leaders will come and see me and bring me a coat.

ACTIVELY LOOKING FOR OPPORTUNITIES

If all we have is truly under God's ownership and we are simply managers, we should actively look for good investment opportunities rather than sit back and wait for appeals. Faithful stewards ask God for wisdom and listen carefully for direction. I've learned that I can count on God's promise to direct me when I ask with a heart that is ready to obey. As a result, I give to ministries because the Lord has prompted me, not because they have approached me with an appeal for money. As we find ministries that faithfully steward the funds entrusted to them, we develop a relationship. That relationship blossoms into a partnership that allows us to invest more resources in the future.

BROADCASTING SEEDS

For a long time I viewed stewardship as simply giving money as generously as possible. I traveled down this path for several years, thinking that I understood my role. I compare it to the image of a farmer casting seed in a field. God gave me seed to cast, and I was supposed to just spread it all over the place.

My initial belief was that the faster and the more I gave away, the better. Picture me taking tons of seed and putting it in the back of a dump truck. So far, so good. But what would you think if I take off down the highway as fast as I can drive, pull the lever, and let the seed fly out of the back? You'd be standing in line to ask, "And how's that working for you?" You know where most of the seed would end up—on the pavement. Not fertile, not smart, and certainly not profitable. But if generosity is the primary goal, maybe I could do better if I went a little faster. Or had a bigger truck.

I thought this was an effective way to distribute God's resources. In the world's eyes, this is how I'd become a generous donor. What I didn't realize is that God has a better way—more efficient and more effective. In God's economy, the number of seeds isn't as much of an issue as their placement.

Rather than a three-foot swath along the side of the highway—not very harvestable, by the way—I could have planted seed like farmers who really know what they are doing. If I would just take a sack of seed and go into a fertile field, I could scatter the seed carefully where God directs. A lot less seed would produce a much greater harvest within God's economy.

The lesson is obvious. I had previously cast too much seed (money) too quickly. Some of it was consumed and wasted. Some of it yielded a harvest along the side of the road, but it wasn't a healthy harvest. On the other hand, I saw that when I strategically sowed money where the Holy Spirit prompted me, there was a great harvest.

Of course it's much easier to broadcast the seed through a dump truck. And it's flashier and more fun than slogging through a field casting by hand. It takes even more time and effort to strategically locate proper fields. Do you really think it's worth it? Just wait till the harvest! It may be easier to fish in your bathtub, but the results aren't very satisfying. So I try to do my homework, put in the effort, listen carefully, and cast by hand. Don't fall for shortcuts. Doing the harder work up front seems to be God's way of doing things. The rewards follow in due time.

PLANT OAKS, NOT MULBERRY TREES

In the 1950s and '60s, many residential developers planted mulberry trees in their new housing subdivisions because they grew fast and provided quick shade. It was an easy way to expedite the landscape of newly constructed homes. But with time, the soft-wooded mulberry trees would crack, split, and become gnarly with suckers growing off the main branches. If the developer did not plant the nonbearing type, the trees would drop mulberries all over the pavement below, leaving nasty stains.

I remember coming into my grandmother's house as a young child with mulberry juice all over my face. "Have you been eating mulberries again?" she asked.

"Who, me? What makes you think that?"

Okay, back to the trees. Oaks, unlike mulberry trees, take a long time to grow. I recently planted two new live oaks in my front yard because my previous trees had been smashed by a tornado. These live oaks will take many years to grow before we benefit from any shade, but they are worth it. Their slow growth contributes to deep root systems that can withstand almost any windstorm. Unless, of course, it's a tornado.

What does this have to do with stewardship? It's all about choices and payoffs. Some pursuits are like planting mulberry trees: quick results, instant gratification, and easy profit. Others require work and patience but yield oak trees of significant stewardship with substantial long-term gains. We know the strength of the oak trees will serve us long after the mulberry trees have collapsed.

INVESTING WITH A STOCKBROKER

After years of investing in financial markets with mediocre returns, I came to the revelation that I was no genius in investing. I have known several stockbrokers and investment advisers over the years. They are always willing to give advice. I have taken much of it and received both good results and poor results. It depends on the broker or the adviser, but most are diligent in their assessment of investment opportunities and honestly communicate their sincere opinions. But when it comes right down to it, I don't want to invest in anything that brokers don't invest in themselves. I now have a philosophy to "put my money where they put their money." Their actions speak much louder than their words.

It's the same way with ministry investment opportunities. Many leaders approach me with great ideas about kingdom opportunities. Most of them are fundraising for projects that support their cause. They are convinced that God has called them to do this work, and they need the funding to accomplish it. Again, like the stockbroker, they are very sincere and mean well. But when a ministry leader approaches me for money to invest in kingdom projects, I simply ask, "Are you investing your own money in this project? Where do you invest?" In other words, as with the stockbroker, I want to invest where the ministry leader invests their own money. Their actions, like a stockbroker's, will speak louder than their words.

GOD REDEEMS EVEN POOR MINISTRY INVESTMENTS

Sometimes I don't see the whole picture. Sometimes ministries have delayed kingdom successes. I've caught myself being critical of how some ministries use money only to find out later that there was great kingdom benefit. I've since learned to be less critical and more attentive while still shrewd in investing with ministries and nonprofits.

I've invested in some good business opportunities and some real failures. I've also invested in ministries that I felt later were a poor investment from my earthly perspective. But by faith I believe God redeems my poor ministry investments when I have sincerely listened to His direction and given in faith. If my heart is to give to Him, He redeems both the offering and the intent. I may not see the return I hoped for in this life, but He has eternity to reveal the true treasure of spiritual returns.

My labor is not in vain if I sincerely work in faith, doing all I know to do when I know to do it. "My beloved brothers, be steadfast, immovable, always abounding in the work of the Lord, knowing that in the Lord your labor is not in vain" (1 Corinthians 15:58).

Chapter 10

RAISING LEADERS, NOT ORGANIZATIONS

Having observed numerous ministries, it is my conviction that God raises men and women of leadership—not necessarily organizations—for His purposes. When these men and women are obedient, they prosper and attract followers. Often a movement or ministry forms around them.

I haven't noticed any biblical accounts of God raising up a ministry and then finding a leader. It always appears to happen in the reverse. Jesus established His church through the apostles, with Peter originally anointed as leader. Although the church will always exist, a parachurch organization, ministry, or movement is certainly different.

I have watched ministries become frustrated when the original founder or leader leaves. Many ministries have a leadership transition plan. Sometimes they work. Other times they do not.

A founder's departure often leads to dysfunction and inefficiencies. The organization's survivors usually have a noble ambition to keep the ministry going. What they often don't realize, however, is the risk of staying in business for business' sake. Without God's anointed man or woman leading the ministry, it can limp along on life support for many years without meaningful results.

On the other hand, if God raises and anoints a new man or woman and the ministry continues around them, results and funding continue naturally. God calls stewards to support the ministry just as he has called and anointed the man or woman of leadership.

I have seen some ministry organizations continue for over a hundred years. Is that a reason to rejoice? Sometimes. Although they have survived leadership transitions, I wonder if some of them should discontinue. Their assets and some of their people might be more effective migrating to other ministries led by anointed men or women.

In our desire to do God's work, we sometimes drift toward the conclusion that any "ministry" with a religious name or a humanitarian ideal is synonymous with God's purpose and blessing. Not necessarily so. If we think holiness accompanies all "ministry" activities, we deceive ourselves. A nonprofit entity is no more holy than a business is unholy. God calls men and women for His purposes. When a business is operated by God's principles and is conducted for God's kingdom, it produces holy results because its leaders are using their gifts to do God's holy work.

I have seen ministries with an outward appearance of being religious while the internal operations and values mirror poorly performing secular businesses. Worse, I've seen some of them mismanaged with dishonesty, discord, and chronic frustration. While allowing for the fact that no one is perfect, we should never create safe havens for ministry leaders to manage outside God's principles. They are held to the same—if not higher—accountability and operational standards as those who are not in ministry.

I love ministries that realize they are called into existence only to do God's work. I find them to have brokenhearted leaders who listen carefully to God speaking through the Holy Spirit and the Bible. These are quite different from ministries with transitioned leaders who are just keeping the organization alive. They may have retained a valid statement of purpose, but their lack of fruit points to ineffectiveness. These leaders beat the bushes for donations to meet their budgets. A good friend of mine calls them "budgetivores." In other words, they eat up their budgets to stay in operation while treading water. What they accomplish is far less than those called by God and supported by stewards.

I meet with numerous ministry leaders on a continual basis. There is an obvious difference between those raised and anointed by God and those who simply fill a ministry position. I strive to associate with those who are conscientious stewards of God's work rather than mere heads of an organization. God calls them to faithfully manage the affairs of the organization with integrity and accountability, but they never lose sight of the higher goal of actually accomplishing God's work.

Although we would be appalled to think that ministry leaders could be less than honest, we have only to look deep in our own heart to see our old nature and what we are capable of doing in a moment of weakness. We see it in leaders who are distracted by the lust of earthly things or who, for a myriad of other reasons, fail to finish strong.

MINISTRY LEADERS AS STEWARDS OF THEIR MINISTRIES

I'm convinced that ministries are entrusted to leaders. The work they are doing must be ordained by God, or it is simply a religious activity, not God's work. Leaders have no right over the ministry except that which is granted to them by God.

The stewards of a ministry not only manage the assets of the ministry but are also accountable to the people under their care. They are responsible for the purpose and direction of the ministry, including its content and the methodology for spreading it. I have observed CEOs delegating financial responsibility, personnel management, and even the direction of the ministry to others. Aimless drifting typically follows. Such CEOs are not sufficiently familiar with the ministry, and the people under them lose productivity and efficiency. There are certain tasks the ministry leader cannot delegate. That is why he or she is called to be the steward.

The ministry leader must also be held accountable for stewarding funds within the ministry. No, this person doesn't have to be the CFO or have an accounting degree, but they must have a sense of the financial direction of the organization. They should be aware of the purposes for expenditures so that waste can be kept at a minimum. Naivety regarding finances is a recipe for financial disaster. So is avoiding involvement with donors and stewards.

It is helpful for the ministry leader to know the staff. They might not know every person, but they must know the key leaders and managers under their charge. The key leaders and managers, in turn, must know the rest of the staff. How can a ministry leader expect to accomplish God's purposes if they don't lead the flock?

I believe God gives anointed ministry leaders a passion. Some call it the "life message." Whatever it's called, it's a message that God has revealed to this leader. I have noticed how wonderfully God has raised up men such as Larry Burkett, Howard Dayton, and Ron Blue in the financial ministry realm and Billy Graham, Luis Palau, Bill Glass, Bill Bright, and Dawson Trotman for evangelism purposes. These men all had definitive, strong messages that were easily communicated and transferred to the masses. Their messages were so divinely strong that they were driven to share life-changing principles and call followers to action.

Men and women called to be stewards of God's resources typically seek ministry leaders who are also stewards. So, when a steward entrusts money to a ministry leader, the steward should be entrusting it to another faithful steward who will then manage those resources within the ministry. This is very similar to the entrusting principle found in 2 Timothy 2:2: "What you have heard from me in the presence of many witnesses entrust to faithful men, who will be able to teach others also." I love the concept that a steward entrusts God's assets to another steward so they can be more effectively used. In fact, I can see that stewardship is much like the discipleship between Paul and Timothy.

Jesus was very clear about this stewardship in numerous parables. The steward always enhanced the asset rather than simply burying (saving) or spending it. A common pattern I have observed, however, is a ministry leader asking, collecting, spending, and then asking for more. The focus on fruit and an increasing harvest is lost in the repetitive loop. I'm sure some would argue this concept, but it has been my observation that faithful stewards lead their ministries to a greater harvest over time.

Money entrusted to a ministry leader can go in two directions. If the ministry leader is not a steward, then the money will probably be used for budgeted expenses and salaries, giving rise to the repetitive loop of "budgeting cycle." On the other hand, if the steward entrusts money to the ministry leader who is also a steward, then that money can continue to grow, bear fruit, and multiply for kingdom purposes.

GOD DOES NOT NEED FUNDING

Marydel and I have been longtime donors to numerous ministries and full-time ministry workers. In my journey of becoming a steward, I've asked God for wisdom and clarity in where to invest His money. I've become convinced that simply giving money to just any Christian organization is neither wise stewardship nor storing treasures in heaven. I've had to go back to the New Testament to determine what Christ said about storing treasures in heaven.

If we truly believe that God owns the world and everything in it, we conclude that He certainly isn't dependent on mortals to fund His work. He already has the resources. If we believe the parable of the talents and other passages regarding stewardship, we conclude that God will resource His work through faithful stewards.

I have recently observed that most nonprofit organizations and Christian ministries have been scrambling to raise funds. But I don't think there is a lack of funding for the work God wants to see accomplished. I remember the motto commonly attributed to Hudson Taylor regarding his organization, the China Inland Mission (now known as OMF International): "God's work done in God's way will never lack God's supply." That old saying rings true, and I feel that God's resources will always be available to fund the work He intends to accomplish. The funding is available, but where are the faithful leaders through whom God can work?

PLAYING THE MINISTRY GAME

As nonprofits and ministries proliferate, the clamor for kingdom dollars intensifies. I understand that not all success is measured by numbers, statistics, or accomplishments and that we can't prove effectiveness by simple metrics of earthly performance. The Lord is the final judge of effectiveness and what is being accomplished for His sake. Nevertheless, as faithful stewards we must do our best to evaluate where to invest because ministries with little effectiveness eat the seed corn of future kingdom harvests.

In my years of investing in the kingdom, I've struggled with inefficient use of donated funds within certain ministries that we support. Some nonprofits and ministries don't perform well. When they lose effectiveness, we should question the reason for their continued existence.

Some ministries seem to exist to employ their large staff even though they accomplish relatively little. Others are unsure of the purpose for their existence or have drifted from their original culture and ethos. Still others are operated for selfish purposes, resulting in dysfunctional internal operations, little accountability, and negligible results. These poor-performing organizations deplete kingdom resources that could be used far more effectively. Time is short. When people's lives and eternal destinies are at stake, our resources should be deployed in the best ways possible.

Profitable businesses develop efficiencies that contribute to their success. These efficiencies require hard work and attention to details so that sloppiness, laziness, and waste do not occur. Constant reexamination of the purpose and tasks of all activities helps ensure they meet the objectives of planned profitability. Simply stated, if an activity doesn't help the bottom line, it is probably not justified. When ministries don't exercise the same discipline, they end up playing the ministry game.

The term *ministry game* may seem unfairly critical, but let me explain what I mean. Nonprofit ministries are formal organizations created to solve an identified problem. Their purpose is not merely to be a fellowship of like-minded people who meet to agree that a problem exists while they talk endlessly about how somebody should do something about it.

People can do a lot of good in the name of Christ at the individual level, up close and personal, without ever forming a legally recognized entity. As long as they are individuals operating under their own authority, they make their own decisions about their motivation, strategy, and level of engagement. And they are individually accountable to God.

When their strategy rises to the level of a formal ministry organization, the organization they form gains the power of multiplied efforts to impact the needs it addresses. It also becomes a serious endeavor, called to God-honoring processes and meaningful outcomes. Both of these require human accountability exceeding that of an individual acting on his own.

A business that solves problems by effectively addressing needs in the marketplace does so through ingenuity and hard work. In the process, its initial investment becomes profitable—a necessary condition for the business's continuing existence. When a nonprofit ministry solves problems by effectively addressing needs, it employs the same kind of ingenuity and hard work—along with the blessing of God's wind in its sails as He inspires stewards to sustain it. The necessary condition for its continuing existence is not financial profitability. Rather, it is the profitability of ministry results. The bottom line is that if the impact does not exceed the inputs, the enterprise should be repaired or retired.

Since nonprofit ministries do not share the responsibility of businesses to be profitable or die, they can be easily lulled to sleep. They can continue going through the motions for a long time without accomplishing anything more than placing a burden on their life support system. A large budget is no guarantee of ministry success, but a budget of any size that is chronically unmet begs this question: Is God indicating that this endeavor has run its course?

The American nonprofit organization is unique in the world. There are no requirements for it to be profitable, run efficiently, or maintain true financial accountability. But in God's economy, everything should be profitable and efficient regardless of the organizational structure. I have observed ministries that were prudent with their expenditures but inefficient with their staff or human resources. Some nonprofit leaders feel they have a higher calling than to be concerned with effectiveness or efficiencies. Why should donors or stewards want to invest in organizations that are not interested in being profitably effective? Organizations that have the most appeal to me have a track record of efficiency and effectiveness. I want to invest in effective causes and organizations that make a difference for eternity.

I think the inefficiencies I've seen in some nonprofits are aggravated when an attitude of cheap grace replaces accountability and discipline. Many Christian organizations I have been involved with seem to look the other way, excusing unacceptable behavior or performance in its team members. I have heard ministry employees ask, "How can they fire me? This is a Christian organization!"

This sense of entitlement is particularly noticeable with those who raise their own support to work within a ministry. Like independent contractors, they see themselves as their own boss. This poses a problem. It is very difficult for a ministry leader to terminate someone who has raised their own support. And unfortunately, without the potential for termination, accountability to the ministry leader sometimes degrades to mere lip service.

Some ministries have outlived their usefulness. Their work can be better accomplished by others. Sometimes a founder's vision cannot be replicated by someone else. Sometimes it seems that God anoints a man or a woman for a specific time. Some founders quit too late. Some are unable to find a leader who can further steward the ministry and culture. Many circumstances can cripple a ministry's viability. Whatever the cause, no ministry should assume a right to continue in perpetuity simply because it can.

TOO MANY NONPROFIT ORGANIZATIONS

In 2021, there were 1.8 million nonprofit organizations in the United States.[8] This is at least one nonprofit organization for every 190 people—outrageous! Why are so many organizations necessary? Where will they get their funding? The proliferation of nonprofits has exploded as younger people enter the nonprofit world as a means to fulfill their desire to make a difference. I appreciate their desire, but all these organizations are seeking funding from generous people.

The designation of "nonprofit" is to allow tax-exempt status. But many people giving to nonprofits don't actually receive the tax benefits they perceive; only a portion of donations are fully deductible on a tax return. And even if they were fully deductible, giving money for nothing more than tax purposes is counterproductive. Giving money to good organizations, however, benefits both the organization and the donor with much more than a mere tax deduction.

As a forty-year investor in the kingdom, I always look for a return on investment. There must be some benefit for giving money away. Why else would I do it? Simply giving money to a nonprofit does not make much sense to me unless there is a defined benefit.

If the US government revokes the opportunity for individuals to receive a deduction on their taxes when giving to a nonprofit, I think it will change the generosity landscape. It could challenge the viability—at least for a while—of some worthy nonprofits. On the other hand, it would definitely serve to clean out laziness and inefficiencies in the nonprofit world. Giving after-tax money would be a strong indication that the donor believes the organization deserves to receive donations.

---

8   Lewis Faulk et al., *Nonprofit Trends and Impacts 2021*, Urban Institute, October 2021, https://www.urban.org/sites/default/files/publication/104889/ nonprofit-trends-and-impacts-2021_2.pdf, 1.

Investing in well-run, efficient organizations makes all the sense in the world—and in God's kingdom.

THE NEW MISSIONARY: THE BUSINESSPERSON

The world is changing in a way that the business place is the new mission field, a wonderful opportunity for evangelism. This paradigm shift is supported by the fact that most people need to work. In most foreign countries, the Christian missionary is no longer welcomed. In quite a departure from previous centuries, many countries now restrict Christian missionaries from entering to evangelize.

With this new paradigm comes a new way of thinking strategically. Business is the new passport into most cultures. As all cultures need good businesses to flourish, Christian businesspeople can be agents for good on many levels. Holy opportunities walk through the doors of real businesses that provide needed goods and services through God's people operating God's way.

When John Enright set up numerous businesses in Africa, he provided a solid business model for the ultra-poor while sharing the abundant life of the gospel. These businesses made him welcome in the African culture as they provided not only employment but also high-quality food. Retained profits expanded the businesses, enabling them to further promote the gospel and provide training for indigenous pastors in the bush.

Not all such attempts in foreign countries will be successful. Business will always be a challenge. Corruption, excessive regulation, and unique foreign business practices all add to the difficulty. But those willing to stick with it can find success at some level to share the gospel and bring abundant life to those they encounter. These business missionaries break the mold of relying on donations as they generate their own income, including margin, in order to share with others.

BUSINESS AS MISSION MISCONCEPTION

"Business as Mission" has become a buzz phrase for evangelism. As Christians, we should always be about the work of the kingdom, whether in full-time ministry or in the business world. Neither is holier than the other. But simply using business as a cover for evangelism is not an effective long-term solution. For example, no one wants a shoddy Christian mechanic telling us about Jesus. We want a good mechanic when our car is broken; forget the evangelism if the car can't be fixed.

A great example of using a business as an economic engine to develop profit and as an opportunity to share God's love and the abundant life involves a tea company in China. For several years Marydel and I supported a young couple to be missionaries in central China upon their graduation from seminary. After learning the language and being involved in cultural adaptation training, they began to engage in their new Chinese community. But things in China started to change. Local authorities were not as friendly toward Christians as they had been at first. It became obvious that China was clamping down on Christian missionaries, requiring most of them to leave the country.

Our friends were not easily deterred. Deciding to be innovative, they started a tea company. To export high-quality boutique teas to the United States, they developed a great website and marketing materials, employed local workers, and began growing tea. This economic engine became profitable enough to pay its employees, but it still required some support from the United States. Marydel and I helped capitalize this company so that the family could stay in-country while ministering to those around them.

Unfortunately, good things don't always last forever. The local authorities finally came to shut down the tea company, requiring this young couple to leave China. The company, although it didn't last for long, served its purpose, and the underlying business was left to be run by locals—a major benefit to them. This was only possible because they managed their company well.

Although Marydel and I did not see a financial benefit from this investment, we know it continues to benefit the Chinese families who still work the tea business.

BUILDING SUSTAINABILITY

Ministries must become financially sustainable if they hope to flourish during turbulent economic times. Ministries that are totally donor reliant may be disappointed when the economy is weak and donors pull back. Sometimes donor resistance is a decision to protect their own well-being or comfort. Sometimes they may have lost their assets and simply do not have the same capacity to give.

Many who go into ministry expect to be funded by other people's money. Capable people in ministry should consider working toward self-sufficiency, depositing money into the kingdom for God's purposes rather than only withdrawing it. A profit model for ministries can move them in the direction of funding their own salaries and expenses in lieu of relying entirely on the donations of others.

I believe that for ministries to be financially sustainable, they must have several characteristics. They must be effective, efficient, and, to the extent possible, local to their area of ministry.

EFFECTIVE

Effectiveness is important because a ministry needs to accomplish a useful purpose. I have observed ministries that seem to exist because of tradition or because they have "always done it this way." It is rarely easy to measure effectiveness in ministry, but it is important to show the fruit of a plan's efforts. Does it work? If not, can it be adjusted to work? Simply being busy does not translate to effectiveness.

It's the same in any business. If a business doesn't have a product or a service to sell to customers who desire it, it will not continue to exist. Any business that simply occupies office space each day doing busy work but not producing anything of value is not effective and will not continue.

Although ministries and nonprofits do not exist to be profit-making enterprises, they *can* generate profitable customer-demanded services. The profits just need to be reinvested into the ministry's efforts to fulfill their stated mission—the reason they were granted nonprofit status to begin with. But regardless of whether they create any financially profitable products or services, they should be profitable in the sense of producing results and creating value. Mere busyness is not a good use of resources.

EFFICIENT

Efficiency is important in any business or ministry. It demonstrates prudence to spend less than is made, resulting in profitability. The efficient use of personnel and resources can mean smaller staffs with higher output.

The biggest potential inefficiency is in personnel. I have observed businesses and ministries alike that have too many people doing too few things. Two or three people doing the work of one is not efficient. Some kinds of work contribute very little to real progress. For example, spending all day making reservations for a trip might make a person look busy, but it could be done more efficiently through a travel professional. Having two or three people in the human resources department of a relatively small firm is probably overkill. Having one person doing multiple kinds of tasks or subcontracting out certain portions of the ministry can enable staff reductions and greater efficiency. What matters is doing work that is crucial to the enterprise.

Efficiency can also be viewed in how expenditures are managed. This doesn't mean buying junk, which can be a different kind of inefficiency, but it does mean ensuring that purchases are necessary and will be used to produce value. In my business, I found a creative solution for otherwise expensive office furniture by using solid-core doors for drafting tables. They lasted well over thirty-five years with a very low initial expense. They didn't go out of style, and they accomplished their intended purpose. If I had bought faddish computer furniture from a typical vendor, it might not have endured years of heavy use.

When it came to computer purchases, we took a different approach. Even though we knew that technology changes rapidly, we bought the best computers available. We understood they would become obsolete in a few years, but we deliberately chose not to skimp here because this was a major tool in the production of our work. Efficiency in expenditures must consider the organization's priorities and a long-term view.

LOCAL

I also look to invest in organizations that are run by people who are local to the area the organization is serving. Local workers have greater knowledge and comfort with the culture and people of their own area. They are almost a necessity for sustainable ministry. This is not to suggest that just any local person will do. I recommend coupling this with finding the most qualified person possible for even the most grassroots jobs. We created proven efficiencies within our organization when we had qualified, high-quality people doing even the smallest of tasks. It resulted in not only needing fewer people but also giving us the highest quality. Details were handled well, and we know from experience that small details affect big projects. Employing local people in ministry also reduces the expenses associated with language training, cultural training, and travel to the field of service.

I think people who are not local can best support a ministry when they have a particular expertise and can then train local people to do that skill within their own ministry. This speeds the pace of the local people's ownership of their ministry and effectiveness in the task.

Marydel and I have supported many ministries that employ mostly local people, and we have seen entrusted resources go much further. For example, we were able to support seminaries in Thailand, Mozambique, and China for the cost of only one US missionary in each country. In effect, we were multiplying the resources, which a foreigner going into a new culture couldn't have done. In other words, money would not have accomplished as much if we had used American (foreign) missionaries as opposed to supporting local people who were properly trained to do their own ministry.

PAUL WORKED TO SUPPORT HIMSELF

I have observed successful ministries moving away from the donor model of support to a financially self-sustaining model. Neither model is the only correct one. I don't find anywhere in Scripture where ministry leaders should be totally supported by others. It appears that the apostle Paul and some other early missionaries were given support. It also appears, however, that they were self-funded to the greatest extent possible.

Paul was the first Christian foreign missionary to share the good news, the gospel of Jesus. Jesus had personally called him on the Damascus road. Tireless and bold, Paul amassed a litany of accomplishments through his hard work. "You remember, brothers, our labor and toil: we worked night and day, that we might not be a burden to any of you, while we proclaimed to you the gospel of God" (1 Thessalonians 2:9).

Paul was the model for working hard in God's kingdom. He was also an outstanding example of not burdening others while doing the work of the gospel. His hybrid approach made him occasionally dependent on the support of others—especially when he was in prison and unable to work—but for the most part he supported himself through his skilled craft. This gave him the added benefit of meeting and building relationships with people in the marketplace.

IT'S A BOTH-AND WORLD

While working with ministries, organizations, and churches, do not think things must be done in only one way. There are several legitimate approaches to funding. The original model was church supported. Missionaries went out from the church and were supported by congregational donations. Many ministries started as church-based missions, including hospitals, retirement homes, and orphanages.

But with time, the church began to relegate its duties to nonprofits and parachurch ministries, giving rise to a reformed model. Ministries and nonprofits began to develop outside the church, raising funds through private individuals, foundations, and other organizations.

In recent years, a for-profit model has emerged. Its common components are sharing the gospel, producing employment, and being profitable. It becomes sustainable while helping the vulnerable and poor with direct aid as well as employment opportunities. For this to be truly effective, there needs to be a partnership among ministry leaders, pastors, and business leaders.

As you may notice, I'm passionate about leaders and not organizations. Organizations would not exist without leaders, and when leaders are not effective, organizations wane. Effective godly leaders raise up the people around them, and their organizations flourish, and the kingdom grows as intended.

Chapter 11

THE CHALLENGES OF FUNDRAISING

It's a reality that doing kingdom work often requires money. Our broken world has no clear answers to the difficulties of fundraising. So many people want to make a difference, and that's a good thing. Unfortunately, they usually want to do it with someone else's money, beginning a cycle of asking for money, receiving donations, spending money, and asking for more. This cycle can be exhausting and frustrating for both the fundraiser and the donor, which can impact everyone's ability to fulfill their call to be stewards.

Effective fundraisers must understand and have answers for the kinds of questions donors ask themselves as stewards. *Will a significant benefit occur because of my contribution? Is this effort really worth the cost? Can I have confidence that the money will be well spent? Is God turning my heart to this ministry? Is there a reward for me? What grade would I give myself as a steward for entrusting the Master's resources to this effort?*

After reading this chapter, I hope donors will see the challenges ministries face as they fundraise while understanding that how and where they give is more important than the dollar amount. I hope that fundraisers will see the questions donors face as they determine how best to steward their funds. Both donors and fundraisers are called to steward the resources God entrusts to them, and together, we can advance the kingdom of God for His glory.

FINDING A GOOD PLACE

As a donor, it is challenging to find a good ministry or nonprofit to send money to. Although nonprofits clamor for money—with the implied assumption that they will achieve great things— some accomplish very little. Unfortunately, ministries don't always provide a good return on investment simply because they operate in the name of Christ.

Many people find this hard to believe, but I know from personal experience that it's difficult to give effectively. Nonprofits and ministries typically think that what they are doing is crucial and that their funding is well deserved. And sometimes they are right. But some recipients lack knowledge, some lack discipline, and others lack effort. Many do not treat donations with the same respect as if they had earned the money themselves—and it shows.

Two key ingredients are necessary for any nonprofit. First, they must strive for excellence in all they undertake, and they should achieve excellence a high percentage of the time. Second, they must be successful in producing outcomes that demonstrate progress. Most investors in organizations or projects want some sort of return. They also want to support something that is successful in accomplishing its intended purpose. When excellence is consistent, success follows.

Some organizations focus on reporting statistics to dramatize a problem that should be addressed. That isn't enough. I want to know what progress is being achieved. Personal commitment and meaningful involvement in a working strategy are huge factors for me in evaluating a ministry and its leadership.

Sometimes ministries are critical of financially wealthy people for not being more generous. Perhaps they would be more generous if they had more opportunity to give with confidence in the effective use of their investment. After all, many wealthy people have earned this money through wise decisions, hard work, and skilled management for good returns. Why would they not want the same kind of diligence when they invest in the kingdom?

Does the kingdom of God need more generous donors or more organizations that are attractive to stewards? Probably both, but I think most stewards are combing the landscape for opportunities to invest in God's kingdom. I don't give money just to get rid of it. I want to see it invested in the kingdom to generate profit for the kingdom.

DO LESS, BETTER

While I want to be generous, I don't want to be perceived as a bad guy for saying no. My general habit has been to say yes most of the time because of Jesus' admonition to give when we are asked. But when I am asked all the time, it puts me on the spot. It's especially hard for me to say no when it's a need I can easily meet. But I'm learning to say no to requests for funding even though they might have great importance to the recipient. If I fund every need for which I'm asked, I'll be doing a hundred things at once and not be effective in any of them. I certainly am not obligated by the Lord to fund everything for which I'm asked. Marydel has encouraged me to do fewer things better as we work to fund God's kingdom, and I'm learning that lesson and developing lasting friendships rather than just cycling through a parade of relationships.

CAN'T FUND EVERYTHING

I'm consistently approached by ministries and nonprofits to fund their efforts. Requests come from direct mailings, media, acquaintances, and friends. I've noticed almost all ministry leaders look to friends as potential donors. This is not wrong, but to expect all your friends to become donors is unreasonable. It certainly makes me uncomfortable at times. Some of my close friends wonder why we don't give to their cause. But we can't fund everything and everybody. We choose to give where the Lord directs us. It doesn't mean that their cause isn't good or that we are critical of it. Sometimes it just means that God will direct others to provide for it.

I don't like the feeling of being a target for fundraisers whenever I develop a relationship with someone in ministry. Almost every new ministry person I meet seems to view me as a potential future donor. Although it may not always be the case, it has made me leery of developing new relationships.

One of my dear friends runs a nonprofit. When I first got to know him, I risked making a frank request: "Please don't ask me for money. I just want to develop a friendship with you without the pressure of not meeting someone's financial expectations." I really respect this guy. He has kept to the request, and we've developed a close friendship. I have given money to his organization out of desire and love for him, but I don't feel obligated to be a continual donor. My genuine friendship with him is more important.

When ministries see financially wealthy people as simply a funding mechanism, they don't understand how to work together in God's kingdom. Asking for too much money or without first establishing a friendship is like reaching too far over a fence. It can feel like reaching prematurely to get peaches off my tree before they ripen.

The constant "ask" by ministry or nonprofit leaders causes me to think they actually believe money grows on trees. Most would never admit it, but they don't think of where the money has come from when they ask. They must realize that it's earned, saved, and often taxed before it can be given, but few seem to consider what goes into the ability to fund organizations. It feels as though wealthy people are looked upon as lucky individuals who happen to have money-bearing trees.

I understand that most ministries are focused on the task at hand and simply need money to accomplish it. But ministry leaders who have been on the mission field and in nonprofits or churches all their careers can easily become desensitized to the plight of donors and how hard it is for them to be profitable.

GOING TO A CHURCH POTLUCK

Going to a church potluck dinner without a dish is sometimes presumptuous and maybe even a bit embarrassing. Everyone at the potluck shows up equal handed, contributing to the welfare of the group for a joyous occasion. But sometimes ministry leaders can be the ones attending without bringing a dish.

What do I mean by this? I've noticed in my years of donating and investing in God's kingdom that some ministry leaders don't consider that they should contribute to their own mission or organization but that they should only ask others to do so. I also sense that many ministry leaders feel like it's their right to be financially supported because they are doing the hard work of ministry. My favorite full-time ministry friends are those who support themselves. Whether through their own resources or by becoming sustainable through other means, they seem to be on equal footing with others when they request support for their cause.

Because of our societal segregation of holy and secular, many ministry leaders feel like gaining support is the best way to go about their work. In the early days, the church sent out missionaries because it was impossible for international missionaries to make a living. This has become the norm for all ministries regardless of whether they are overseas or could have the ability to generate their own income, but it doesn't have to be this way. By building economic engines to sustain their ministries, they give back to the kingdom more than they take out, benefitting the poor economically as well as spiritually.

Notwithstanding all I have said about the appeal of self-sustaining kingdom work, I wholeheartedly believe that some ministries should focus entirely on spiritual returns and do it very well. When they are diligent to evangelize or disciple effectively, they build the kingdom with a return on investment that will not be known until we reach heaven. I take joy in investing in these organizations, especially when they have a wise steward at the helm.

In the cases when fundraising is required, the question is how these fundraisers can achieve their goals while honoring donors. I love what Henri Nouwen said in his book *A Spirituality of Fundraising.* Fundraising is actually a ministry and a holy activity when done right. To be effective, fundraisers must be sincerely passionate about what they are doing. Especially meaningful to me was the idea that fundraisers need to approach donors with the donors' best interests in mind—looking for the benefit for the donor and not just a transaction to feed the ministry.

I relate this to a man who finds treasure in a field and is so excited that he sells everything to buy it. He also invites his friends to come along and help him purchase it because it is so valuable. He wants to share with his friends the great potential wealth he has found. This happens when I ask others to invest in the things that I find valuable. I sometimes think to myself, *I've found something I believe in and am excited about—something I think is extremely important for God's kingdom. I would like my friends to join me in it. Their assets will help buy this field, and we can mine the treasure together.*

I believe stewardship includes entrusting assets to other faithful stewards. Since stewardship is akin to discipleship in many respects, godly stewardship from donors requires finding faithful leaders within ministries. Godly stewardship from ministry leaders requires diligently handling the funds they're given. This is how we can all bring a dish to the table.

IS YOUR CAUSE REALLY WORTH IT?

All good ministry leaders believe their cause is worth what they are asking. I've had some boldly ask me for a million dollars. I think it's safe to say they don't have any idea what it takes for me to donate a million dollars. Let me explain.

Marydel and I donate money we have saved. This money is saved from salary and profits I received from the economic engine of my architectural firm. To generate profit, I depend on the performance of employees. Most of the money I've accumulated over my lifetime was earned hourly by providing professional services through my employees—not through a windfall. For me to make a donation, I have to run a company efficiently, earn a profit, pay taxes, and save.

For a nonprofit or ministry to ask me for a million dollars is a lot. They don't realize that for me to donate this amount requires the profit generated by one man or woman working for me for over twenty years. In the back of my mind I'm thinking, *How would that employee feel if I gave his or her hard-earned profit away for this cause?*

You should see the expressions I get when I ask ministry leaders that question. Eyes glaze over and sometimes mouths hang open. They had no idea. So I ask them again, "Is what you're asking really worth one of my architect's entire career at my firm?" Once they recover, they usually say, "Yes." And I ask,

"Really?" If after careful consideration I believe it really is, I gladly make the donation with great joy. But it's a weighty decision.

THE PROBLEM WITH OTHER PEOPLE'S MONEY

The sad truth is that many people don't spend other people's money with the same diligence as they spend their own. It's easy to see why. You can't always see the time and effort it takes to make that money. But if you don't handle other people's money well, who would ever trust you to handle your own? Jesus talked about this in Luke 16: "One who is faithful in a very little is also faithful in much, and one who is dishonest in a very little is also dishonest in much. If then you have not been faithful in the unrighteous wealth, who will entrust to you the true riches? And if you have not been faithful in that which is another's, who will give you that which is your own?" (vv. 10–12).

What makes an organization think they should be given more if they don't handle current donations properly? To be casual or careless is one of the biggest affronts to donors. For example, I've known a ministry to make reservations on an airline just days before the trip. If they were doing it for themselves to go on vacation, I can assure you they would make it a month or more in advance to get the lowest and best fare. Donors and ministry workers striving to do God's work should feel sad that valuable kingdom funds were wasted due to poor planning.

Some people believe that as long as a purchase fits into the budget, the funds used have been well stewarded. But while budgets serve a valuable purpose, sometimes they can lead to casual rather than frugal purchases. Just because a budget gives an estimate for an expenditure does not mean we shouldn't exercise care in finding good value. I learned from my experience working for Walmart, the largest US retailer, that no matter what the budget, I needed to get the most economical price on everything. Walmart's profitability was significantly affected by its ability to cut its overhead cost. Little things add up to big profits. Walmart's philosophy made them successful and profitable. Ministries and donors alike could learn a lot from them as they work together to maximize the effect of every dollar.

UNINTENDED CONSEQUENCES OF FUNDRAISING

As stewards within God's kingdom, we have a sense of duty to deploy assets, tithes, offerings, and donations where we feel led. Ministries need money, and they look to donors to provide it. Many times, organizations, ministries, churches, and even individuals can be unintentionally aggressive in seeking funds. Ministries in difficult times run harder and chase after generous donors faster. It sometimes seems as though the attitude is "We'll go do the ministry if we can get the money" instead of "We'll do the ministry regardless of the money." The consequences of this attitude are the dependence on donors rather than God, and many times, I have felt unappreciated and even taken advantage of. These may be my own feelings, but let me share a bit more about how I have felt in the past.

Sometimes I have felt like an ATM for individuals or ministries to come back to year after year to grab additional funds for their projects. It can feel like the money is just supposed to magically come out of some slot when the right buttons get pushed. This may sound harsh, but I'm sure many donors have felt this way when the "ask" is simply predicated on the previous year's generosity. Some ask, "Can you do what you did last year?" or "How about increasing your faith by giving a little more?"

Fundraisers may see someone's generosity as an indication that they have a desire to continually fund. With some donors in some situations, that may be true. Other times, donors may want to give generously without feeling continually obligated to do the same in the future. Remember that as faithful stewards, we are giving where God wants us to give for the benefit of the kingdom. Fundraisers sometimes push people to the point that they just don't want to deal with them any longer. When donors don't really believe in the mission but feel hounded by solicitations or want to be polite, they pay money for the sole purpose of avoiding more requests—at least for the moment. But both fundraisers and donors have to question if this really gives God glory or builds the kingdom.

RELATIONAL VERSUS TRANSACTIONAL FUNDRAISING

People hired by ministries, nonprofits, and churches as fundraisers have a tough position. They look at everyone as a potential donor, and they can't help but develop relationships with the hope of raising money at a later date. This is not wrong. This is part of their job, and if they don't do it well, they won't keep it very long. But when everyone in their sphere of influence is a candidate for funding them, it makes relationships difficult.

The need for donors can easily lead to one of the ugly truths in relationships with fundraisers. Most fundraisers and individuals raising financial support pursue relationships because they don't want to make a transactional "ask." But to develop a relationship with the primary purpose of raising money is not much different.

When fundraisers want relationships so they can go deeper with donors, I get it. I have been involved in many of those relationships. But if the relationship is for the purpose of raising funding for their ministry, you have to question whether it is truly an in-depth relationship. Motive still matters. It seems more like a transactional relationship that just appears to be a friendship. As my wife says, "They aren't your friends. They really just want your money."

Most people working in ministry and nonprofits do not want to hear any notion that their relationship is all about the money. But it has been my experience that the motivation behind many ministry and donor relationships is the fundraising. Absent the fundraising need, the relationship would not deepen. This can be quite disconcerting among generous donors who are relied upon to provide for these ministries. Sometimes unhealthy relationships develop, characterized by codependency and resentment or fatigue in the donor. I once had a ministry leader tell me that I had donor fatigue, that I just wasn't joyful in my giving. That really bothered me, particularly since their persistent request for funds was tiring me. The relationship revolved around only what I could do for them. Part of a true friendship is recognizing that God speaks to all of us differently and that we need to both listen to His call and respect others as they follow His call for them.

For the rest of this chapter, I am going to share some of the fundraising techniques I have seen used that treat my relationship with a ministry as a transaction before closing with some steps I have taken to build true relational partnerships with ministries. If you are a ministry leader, take note of how certain fundraising techniques can discourage donors and potentially harm the kingdom. If you are a donor, examine your own relationships with organizations to ensure that distractions or weariness isn't keeping you from God's mission for you.

IS IT REALLY THE LAST CHANCE?

On one particular Giving Tuesday not long ago, I received thirty-seven emails requesting funding. While I think it's a good idea to encourage people to be generous, the constant emails manufactured pressure. They informed me that I had only a few more hours to give, as though it's a game with a final buzzer. Being given "last chances" to donate can shout, "We desperately need your money! And we're okay with using gimmicks to get it." These can come in the form of matching gifts, challenge gifts, or the statement that time is running out for this giving opportunity.

I don't like to be given one last chance—with only minutes left to give. The artificial deadline can play on emotions and doesn't allow people the option to prayerfully consider where God is calling them to give.

GOING THROUGH THE JUNK MAIL

Every day we receive loads of junk mail and marketing emails. It can be overwhelming, but if we indiscriminately trash all mail, we risk missing something important. Carefully sorting through it all is a growing intrusion. Recipients get better and more automatic at tuning it out, resulting in many requests from good ministries just routinely getting thrown away. While I think solicitations are necessary for some ministries and most nonprofits to survive, the bold ask is sometimes frustrating to me as a donor. The time and energy it takes to sort through the requests could distract us from nudges by the Holy Spirit and could be used to do the kingdom work God has called us to do, like strengthening relationships with people in the ministry or organization.

CHRISTMAS ENVELOPES

When ministry leaders send out their Christmas cards, I am excited to find out how they are doing. Sometimes I see an extra envelope inside, and I hope to find money in it just like I did as a little kid. When I was growing up, if I got an envelope at Christmas, it usually meant that my parents or grandparents had put cash in it. But quite to my disappointment, most envelopes I receive at Christmas from missionaries are not gifts; they are asking me for money.

Sometimes I have concluded that the reason an envelope is stuffed in a Christmas greeting is a bit of laziness: *Let's kill two birds with one stone. Wish them a Merry Christmas and use the opportunity to raise year-end support.* I realize that fundraising is very important and usually done at the end of the year. Most people seem to do their charitable giving at the last minute. I don't want to sound like a bah-humbug, but I'm tired of being solicited with a Christmas card. My generosity is not stimulated by the Christmas season. My advice to missionaries and ministry people is to wish everyone a Merry Christmas. That is enough. That touch will remind people that, yes, they are still on the mission field, and yes, they still need your support. If someone wants to give at that time, they can figure out how to get it to you.

Handwritten notes and letters are always read and cherished. If that sounds old-school, just do it for your older donors. I just recommend not sending your Christmas greeting by email since typing one email and sending it to hundreds of people doesn't build the relational connections God uses to build the kingdom.

PARTNERSHIP WITH MINISTRIES

Some ministry leaders appear to have an attitude that says, "Give us the money, and we'll do the work. Please don't meddle. You do your job of giving, and we'll do the rest." This is not a very effective invitation to partnership.

Others are eager to call their donors "partners." I can understand why. Donors want to feel special, and ministries want to make them feel that way. But just because I give a ministry money does not make me a partner with them. I'm still just a donor unless our relationship expands into a true partnership.

True partners share the burden of risk and the benefits of reward together. Merely giving money doesn't necessarily result in either risk or reward. Most ministries and nonprofits will probably argue that point with me. I'm sure some people feel like they are in a partnership because they donate. I understand that not all risks and rewards are financial; some are spiritual, and some are emotional, but unless there is a risk-reward factor, I don't see simple donations as a serious form of partnership.

I think a more holistic partnership between various roles in the venture is a better way for each to fulfill its contribution. Ministry leaders manage the hands-on work, churches support it, and business leaders give their management expertise and capital. Each has an important part to play. Working effectively in God's kingdom requires partnership with other faithful stewards. This partnership is a hybrid of both business and ministry leaders.

As in many business partnerships, there are typically two types of partners. One partner may take an equity (ownership) position by providing capital or financial assets, while the other provides sweat equity by managing the daily work. Both are equally vital although they have different roles. The sweat equity partner is working hard at the current tasks at hand. The financial equity partner had previously worked hard to develop the knowledge and skills necessary to create the invested capital—knowledge and skills that may have some crossover benefit for the sweat equity partner wise enough to tap into it. Neither partner can function without the other. It is just like the apostle Paul's analogy of the body in 1 Corinthians 12:12–26. The hand is not more important than the foot nor the eye more important than the mouth. A properly functioning body requires all parts to work together in coordination.

How is this different from the attitude I mentioned earlier—the "Give us the money, and we'll do the work" attitude? The difference may be subtle, but it is significant. Financial equity partners have a real interest in the outcomes and impact of the venture. And they may have valuable counsel to offer. Sweat equity partners should be open to their ideas and treat them with respect. Financial equity partners must keep in mind that not every business principle or strategy is a perfect fit for ministry and that being an expert in one does not make them an expert in the other. Both need to sincerely honor the other. It's respect. It's humility. It's partnership. It's God's design. It's beautiful.

FRIENDS INVESTING TOGETHER

After years of struggling to know where best to give, distracted by the constant noise of fundraising efforts, I am beginning to see a better way. My best friends and partners in ministry are those who are also stewards. Stewards are usually directed by the Holy Spirit and prompted where to give. Not only is the ministry opportunity revealed but the timing and amount as well. Stewards work in harmony with the needs of God's kingdom.

We invest relationally with other stewards. Sometimes we invest with other friends who have found a good investment opportunity, whether in a business or a nonprofit. Sometimes the business may just provide good jobs for people or produce needed goods or services. And, of course, we also prioritize investing in efforts that directly benefit the poor.

We're not so interested in making money just to give it to others to spend. Our preference is to make or do things to build God's kingdom *and* turn a profit so money can then be reinvested. Although the idea is attractive, it's not easy. The opportunities are scarce.

Having journeyed through much of the world with several wonderful stewards, I've experienced true comradery as we have discussed our kingdom investments and chosen to pursue some of them together. I would much rather invest with stewards than simply give money for others to use.

I found that the easiest way to work in kingdom partnerships is with my friends. We develop friendships that are neither one-sided nor based on a particular expectation. Instead, we relish the comradery of working in the same direction: building God's kingdom. It doesn't always have to be all about money.

Chapter 12

LIFE IS HARD, AND TIME IS SHORT

Life is hard. Business is hard. Learning to be effective as a steward in God's kingdom is a journey. And not an easy one.

Good stewardship is as hard as creating the assets to begin with. Many financially wealthy men and women struggle to successfully steward money into nonprofits and ministries. Living with the expectation that life, our work, and our stewardship are rewarding but hard is an important step toward working effectively in God's kingdom.

BUILDING ECONOMIC ENGINES IS JUST PLAIN HARD

The easy is commonplace. Anything of any value requires effort. Building economic engines is not like instant oatmeal. It's more like trying to score a goal in a thick fog. It takes commitment and perseverance, two words that remind me of early-morning high school football practices—especially the two-a-days when afternoon heat was stifling. Or running five miles to I-35 and back before wrestling practice. Or rising at 5:15 a.m. to run around White Rock Lake regardless of the weather. It's sticking with something without an apparent, immediate reward. But it's for a season as you trust God for the big picture because you can't see everything all at once—only the parts of the plan He chooses to reveal in any given moment.

Building an economic engine required me to drive thirty-five hundred miles in seven days while looking at thirty-five old Walmart stores with my seven-year-old son. It was working so hard in a season of life that I wasn't home to mow my grass in the daylight. But then again, it was just for a season.

It took a long time to build an effective and efficient architectural firm as a sustainable economic engine, but God empowered it for the purpose of helping fund His kingdom and to develop other economic engines. We all want to see a return on investment, but success is not always determined by early results. Sometimes the breakthrough we need is one strategic adjustment away.

NO EASY WAY THROUGH

In a fallen, broken world, easy ways out exist everywhere. But they never get us to a future we want, only to a future in which we will look at the past with regret. We don't want a way *out*; we want a way *through*. A way through the obstacles, the confusion, the discouragement. We know that people are broken, our family is broken, things we do in life are broken, but God can redeem our brokenness and use it for good. We want to get to the other side, the place where we know we have done our best for His kingdom.

God's pattern throughout Scripture is to choose ordinary people for extraordinary purposes. Stewards in God's kingdom are men and women who submit to the authority of Christ and whose lives are characterized by humility. This unique condition rarely occurs apart from being broken by God in order to rise to a higher level of purpose. This is the seed dying to give birth to a tree, ultimately producing future seeds and trees beyond number.

We were not guaranteed an "easy street" at salvation. In fact, the apostle Paul said that we should expect persecution and hardship. The apostles epitomized serving God's kingdom while suffering. I think we have been misled to think that once we accept Jesus, following Him will be easy as we get magically transported to the good life. Not so. Instead, we find ourselves in enemy territory, always in a battle and always under attack. The more effective we are in God's kingdom, the more acute the attack by spiritual forces of evil.

Should that tempt us to give up and look for a way out? Never! "You, dear children, are from God and have overcome them, because the one who is in you is greater than the one who is in the world" (1 John 4:4 NIV).

Don't look for a way out; look for the way through. Embrace hardships in life knowing that they are part of the process of making us complete, mature, perfect, well-equipped workers in God's kingdom. Pray for the ability to endure, to have gratitude for past blessings, and to be hopeful for the future. "We can rejoice, too, when we run into problems and trials, for we know that they help us develop endurance. And endurance develops strength of character, and character strengthens our confident hope of salvation. And this hope will not lead to disappointment. For we know how dearly God loves us, because he has given us the Holy Spirit to fill our hearts with his love" (Romans 5:3–5 NLT).

URGENCY

I sense that I don't have a lot of time left. This feeling provides a sense of urgency. I can't explain why I have this feeling, but I know that the Lord is nudging me to pick up the pace in conducting His business. I have come up with a series of phrases to help me be diligent to complete the tasks before me.

1. Life is too short to drink bad coffee. Quality and excellence in everything I do is like drinking very good coffee. I hate lukewarm, bitter, or bland coffee. It makes me want to spit it out.

2. Life is too short to drink cheap beer. Too often I settle for less. A past experience with cheap beer made me sick. I want to maintain high standards while striving to do my very best.

3. Life is too short to listen to bad music or watch boring movies. There is so much that is so much better: enjoying God's beautiful creation, focusing on wonderful relationships with those around me, prioritizing the truly good things in life rather than the counterfeits.

4. Life is too short to carry a heavy backpack. I can't allow the burdens of this world to rob me of my high calling. Encumbrances can take many shapes including unhealthy relationships, debt and other financial obligations, lifestyle excesses, and hobbies that distract from eternal priorities.

5. Life is too short, so drive a rental. Being too attached to my possessions impedes my ability to be free from worry. I can't afford to be always worried about the first ding on a new car. A rental mentality places more importance on utility, allowing me to focus more on important tasks.

A DAYDREAM OF EXTRAORDINARY TIMES AHEAD

I once daydreamed about a tsunami warning.

At first, the scene was perfection, the kind captured in travel brochures that reality can never quite match. Sunshine on a sandy beach with azure waves teasing the feet of children building sandcastles. Perfect air and water temperatures, low humidity, a gentle breeze, and no bugs. Dads in waist-deep water launching squealing kiddos into the air. Moms lounging under a sun umbrella with a napping baby, a cool drink, and a new novel. Perfection.

Earlier in the day a potential warning had been squeezed into late-breaking news. Most of these folks hadn't paid attention. They were too eager to get their vacation day started at the beach. Who could blame them? The afternoon wore on and the crowds kept building. No one seemed to have a clue that danger was on the way and nothing could stop it.

The shifting of tectonic plates three thousand miles away had created a huge seismic shudder. Now a massive wall of water was soundlessly speeding toward this beautiful beach. No clouds, no rain, no high winds, no crashing surf, no apparent threat. Just a silent but crushing wave out in the open sea, bearing down on clueless vacationers who had no idea today would be their last. Yes, there were warnings, but too few were listening.

Startled at this crazy melodrama of a daydream, my brain began to search for parallels. It didn't take long. Our American culture and economy are unraveling before our eyes. But the water still feels good, and the sun is nice. No one can see the wall approaching. Too many distractions keep us preoccupied. We're getting used to the polarization of our society and a dysfunctional government that has left its Judeo-Christian roots. Anchorless people demanding to live their own truth—which changes as fast as fashion—are completely unaware that they are drifting in the path of a tsunami.

It won't take much bad economic news to turn us toward desperation. I hear approaching whispers of the mantra now: *The government will take care of us. Just trust their new digital financial system. The old rules don't apply anymore. This is a new age.* And in the process, we dismantle the free enterprise that has rewarded spiritual values, honest work, and creative energy to build the greatest nation on earth.

Then I imagine more than just the abstract concept; I see concrete details of a not-too-distant future.

Imagine this scenario: My wife goes to fill her gas tank. Standing at the pump, she calls me at the office. "My credit card isn't working at this pump," she says, "so I tried a different card. It didn't work either. I even tried our ATM card. No deal."

I stay calm. After all, it isn't happening to me. "Did you talk with someone inside?"

"Yes, the lady doesn't know why there's a problem. All she said was several other people complained about the same thing. 'But our systems are up and running just fine,' she says."

Becoming desperate, my confused wife puts in twenty dollars of gas because that is all the cash she has with her. I slump back into my chair, puzzled. Wondering why our credit cards aren't working, I take the next logical step and call the bank to see what is wrong.

Our banker is cordial but uncharacteristically distant. Finally, she says, "Well, your account is frozen."

"What do you mean frozen? By whom?"

"Not us. At least not as far as I can tell. It's not our fault. Maybe it's the IRS. Are you behind on taxes?"

"No, I'm not behind on taxes. I'm not behind on anything. This can't be happening."

Softening her tone a little, she says, "You're the third person to call this morning with the same kind of problem. I don't know what to say. I am so sorry, but when I look online, I am denied access to your account. Somehow we've been shut out."

So there I sit at my desk realizing that it is all coming true. We are kicked out of "the system" that is supposed to "take care of us." We are no longer able to use our credit cards, bank accounts, debit cards, or investment accounts—all because six months earlier I'd refused to sign some required documents for a new electronic currency system. I had wanted to hold out because I just didn't think it was right for the government to have electronic access to all our assets. I felt privacy was important and that I still had my constitutional rights. Apparently not.

Now what are we to do? Unable to use our out-of-the-system financial accounts, cash is the only option left. But rumor has it that the government is making cash obsolete in favor of the new electronic currency. Our decimated economy is in a massive seizure following a stream of desperate executive orders.

As many thoughts collide, I get another call from my wife. She says, "We really need to fill up the car. Do you have any cash at the house?"

"Yes, look in the safe," I say with a forceful exhale. I'd had enough of this daydream for one day. Shaking it off, I prayed, *God, help us.* I'm not sure I ever meant it more.

This may be a fictitious scenario, but can you imagine the layers of fear ahead if something like this were to occur? More than ever we need to take God's call seriously: "Trust in the LORD with all your heart, and do not lean on your own understanding. In all your ways acknowledge him, and he will make straight your paths" (Proverbs 3:5–6).

We now have our financial tsunami warning. We are told to prepare ourselves but not to lose heart. So how are we to respond? The Master will return, and his servants should be found faithfully utilizing what has been entrusted to them so they can take care of those on His heart. (Review Jesus' words in Matthew 24:45–47 and 25:34–40.)

The Bible instructs faithful stewards in their preparation for the end times. They are to be like the bridesmaids preparing their lamps awaiting the bridegroom described in Matthew 25:1–13. In this parable, the wise bridesmaids prepared their lamps with extra oil and awaited the bridegroom. The foolish bridesmaids, however, did not bring extra oil. Unprepared when the appropriate time came, they were unable to enter the wedding banquet.

Wise stewards know they must prepare to be effective in executing their duties. They are to look for opportunities to invest, manage, and deploy talents and assets where the Holy Spirit directs. The effectiveness of stewards is directly tied to their obedience.

Although we don't know the exact hour, we can heed the current tsunami warnings as we approach extraordinary days. Let's do it together while we still have time.

Chapter 13

KINGDOM TREASURES

A MARKET FREEFALL

There is no guaranteed safe place to put money. I learned that lesson well in 1987 when the stock market crashed on an October afternoon. The freefall of stocks was the greatest decline since the Great Depression. Panic spread throughout the financial markets as investors, retirees, and nearly everyone lost a significant part of their assets in a single day.

I was one of the lucky few. I had previously transferred all my stocks out of the market to a cash position in August when the market seemed to be too good to be true. I was able to preserve my gains and avoid the slaughter that followed. But it scared me to see how quickly the value of assets could drop.

I had been fortunate once, but I realized how futile it was to try to use common sense to avoid future financial disasters. Since I have no crystal ball and no way of really knowing what goes on behind the financial scenes, I'm at the mercy of what seem like whimsical fluctuations. Even cash in the bank is subject to the stability of that bank. In 2008, many banks and financial institutions fell. I considered overseas currencies and stocks, but again, fluctuations in currencies and foreign countries going bankrupt did not give me confidence. I tried commodities. Well, we know that's risky. On a good day, gold is fun, but you can also lose your shirt. Ditto with silver. To add to this problem, hyperinflation has devastated many countries in the past. And it may be on the horizon in the US economy. With our mounting debt, lack of discipline to save, and pressure from foreign economies, hyperinflation is a serious threat. Savings lose value and actually become worthless over time as their buying power erodes in the face of rapidly increasing prices.

With all this uncertainty, I wondered, *Where can I put money so that it will be safe?* My conclusion? Earthly money will never be totally safe. Maybe it's not even supposed to be.

According to Jesus, the only safe place to store treasure is in heaven. Marydel and I decided to build our financial portfolio with investments we intended to become treasures in heaven. We began to consciously invest in things important to God. I soon realized that giving money wasn't the only criterion for storing treasures. Good stewards invest intelligently in things God values.

Don't interpret this to mean that I'm opposed to savings and investments. I save and invest regularly, but I refuse to rely on those—or any earthly asset—for my security. I don't think God ever intended anything on earth to be completely secure; even the earth itself is doomed to pass away and be replaced by a new one. The shining option for us as faithful stewards is distributing investments as God prompts. I am convinced that these will be waiting when I need them.

HOW DO WE KNOW OUR TREASURES ARE IN HEAVEN?

A crowd of many thousands had gathered and Jesus began to teach them. He said, "Sell your possessions and give to the poor. Provide purses for yourselves that will not wear out, a treasure in heaven that will never fail" (Luke 12:33 NIV). "Store up treasures for yourselves in heaven, where moth and rust do not destroy, and where thieves do not break in and steal. Because where your treasure is, there your heart will be also" (Matthew 6:20–21 EHV).

On another occasion, Jesus was speaking to a rich ruler who asked how to inherit eternal life. Jesus replied, "Sell everything you have and give to the poor, and you will have treasure in heaven. Then come, follow me" (Luke 18:22 NIV).

Do you want your righteousness to endure forever? "He [who] has given to the poor; his righteousness endures forever" (Psalm 112:9). Do you want to lend to the Lord? "Whoever is generous to the poor lends to the Lord, and he will repay him for his deed" (Proverbs 19:17). Throughout the Gospels, Christ talked about giving to the poor who were disadvantaged, unrepresented, helpless, defenseless, as well as the widows, orphans, prisoners, and those without the ability to take care of themselves. When we help the poor, we receive God's rich blessings for eternity.

Christ instructs us to put our treasures in heaven in lieu of accumulating them on earth. But how can we be certain our treasures make it to heaven? This journey of discovery has led me to believe that although giving money to the poor is a precious activity that ensures treasures in heaven, there are many ways to give, and some are better than others.

I enjoy building economic engines that make money to serve the poor. Although I am not personally effective in feeding the poor or clothing the naked, I can entrust money to those who are. This is why I like giving to nonprofits, ministries, and charities that know how to do those things well. It's more effective. If they can spend my money for God's kingdom better than I can, then I joyfully give it to them.

Since simply giving money is not necessarily a holy activity, it's made me wonder how giving ensures that our treasures are in heaven. What happens if those receiving the money don't use it wisely? What if they waste it? Some organizations imply that if we just give them our money, our treasures will be in heaven. But I don't buy it. I don't think simply giving money for a cause or being a philanthropist makes you any holier than building a business that becomes an economic engine to help others. Anyone with money can be a philanthropist. God will judge my heart's intentions and redeem my actions. I retain a stewardship responsibility that is not best exercised by simply giving money.

Sometimes it doesn't make sense to give. When hard work and business efficiency produce profits to share, why give those profits to an organization that does not share the values that produced it? How do we explain to our employees—the people who helped generate the profits—that our donated funds may not be used with frugal diligence? Will my employees be proud of how I used the profit they made for God's kingdom?

Holy giving is more than simply giving. It is stewarding resources as directed by God. If we truly believe that God is the owner of all our assets, then it is His responsibility to prompt us where, when, and how much to give. The Spirit confirms the amount, the timing, and the recipient. I stand in amazement at how often this alignment comes in concert with the recipient's needs. When money is well stewarded, everything about it is holy. That is when the treasures are stored in heaven. And that is when our heart leans toward God's kingdom "on earth as it is in heaven" (Matthew 6:10).

GENEROSITY IS NOT THE GOAL

I am learning to become generous with most everything I own. Some of the things I've done may be considered weird or outrageous, but I've felt compelled to do them anyway. On one occasion I gave the shirt off my back to a coffee shop owner in Capital Reef National Park and on another, a fellow at the Nebraska State Fair. Thank goodness I was wearing a T-shirt underneath! I gave my favorite company jacket to a dear friend, and my favorite sports jacket to a ministry leader at lunch one day. I generally give books out of my bookshelf to anyone interested. If someone compliments a tie I'm wearing, I quickly shuck it and hand it to him. On three different occasions, I've given valuable artwork to dear friends because of my affection for them, despite it making no economic sense as a return on investment. I say all this not to brag but to demonstrate how far I've had to go to develop a generous spirit while tearing my heart away from my favorite possessions.

Generosity is a large part of stewardship, but it is not the primary goal. A person can be generous without being a good steward. Generosity, however, softens our hearts toward the things of the kingdom and those in need. It's a great place to begin our journey toward stewardship because God wants us to have generous souls.

If the generosity movement were to focus only on loosening the pocketbooks of donors, it could never fulfill the total purpose of stewardship. In some cases, giving generously to an organization may be wasting money within God's kingdom. Effectively placing funds is one of stewardship's most important functions. Faithful stewards listen and obey, enabling God to redeem their contributions.

There was a culture of generosity in the time of Jesus. There was also a culture of giving to the poor as exemplified many times in Jesus' actions on their behalf and in His parables. He taught

His disciples to give to the poor. Even at the last supper when Judas was getting ready to betray Christ, the disciples assumed that he was leaving to give money to the poor, something they routinely did.

THE BEST TWENTY DOLLARS I'VE SPENT IN A WHILE

When in Colorado Springs in 2018, I went to a Walgreens drugstore to pick up a couple of things. When I came out, a homeless man named Ryan was standing there. I don't remember if he politely asked me for money or if I just sensed that he needed something. I started to give him a couple of dollars, and then I was prompted by the Holy Spirit: *Why not just give him a twenty?* Call me crazy! When I handed it to Ryan, he beamed and then asked for my name and shook my hand. We talked a few more minutes, and he gave me another handshake and a fist bump. There was true joy and elation in his eyes. I don't know Ryan's story, but in our brief encounter he said he was an army veteran and hard luck had found him.

Many don't believe that giving money to homeless people is prudent. I understand. But if you could have seen the joy in his face, it certainly felt like it came from heaven. Who knows, he might even have been an angel giving me an opportunity to store a little treasure in heaven.

WHAT ARE HEAVENLY TREASURES?

Understanding the great mystery of how you practically store or "lay up" your treasures in heaven required you to determine what these treasures are.

Look carefully at what is considered a treasure. We naturally think of things that occupy a special place in our heart, something we value highly because of how it makes us feel. This includes money (with its promise of power and security) and possessions (with their promise of status and comfort or their sentimental value). I noted while reading through the book of Proverbs that components of righteous character are also treasures: wisdom, faithfulness, love, righteousness, humility. The Gospels teach that deeds done for the glory of God are certainly treasures as well, leading me to believe that doing good works accomplishes two important things: it develops our righteous character and lays up treasures in heaven.

We can't comprehend what treasure in heaven looks like or even whether any of it is physical. Paul, who tells us in 2 Corinthians 12 of visiting "the third heaven" (v. 2), also tells us that "no eye has seen, nor ear heard, nor the heart of man imagined, what God has prepared for those who love him" (1 Corinthians 2:9). We know our earthly assets don't follow us after death, but Jesus' parables imply a link between our management of them and our reward in heaven. What we can know for certain is that if Jesus, the Creator of the universe, talks about treasure in heaven exceeding anything on earth, it is something we don't want to overlook, undervalue, or miss.

KINGDOM CURRENCY

Now let's shift the conversation away from our future home to think instead about God's kingdom here on earth. This is the part we can see and over which we have control.

What do we do with earthly assets that are always at risk and have only temporal value at best? How do we convert them into assets that God can use for His purposes in His kingdom now? I think it's safe to assume that if we can get this part right, we will have treasure in heaven. So let's take a closer look at asset conversion.

In any economic system, assets are items of value that must be converted to a common currency in order to transfer, exchange, or redeem them. I might have a wealth of assets but unless I have a means to convert them into a usable currency, their value is locked up and unavailable to help me.

In a similar way, earthly wealth is unavailable for kingdom use unless it can be converted to a tradable currency. What is that kingdom currency?

KINGDOM ASSETS

Before answering the currency question, let's try to understand what *kingdom assets* are. An easy example is wisdom. Solomon declared over and over again that wisdom far exceeds physical assets. "Blessed is the one who finds wisdom, and the one who gets understanding, for the gain from her is better than gain from silver and her profit better than gold. She is more precious than jewels, and nothing you desire can compare with her" (Proverbs 3:13–15).

Other nonphysical assets include faith, hope, and love, along with joy, peace, patience, kindness, goodness, faithfulness, gentleness, and self-control. God's Word is certainly a kingdom asset, along with the souls of precious men and women who belong to God through faith in Jesus. Kingdom assets are crucial in God's economy because He values them, provides them for us, directs our use of them, and blesses the world through them.

MAKING THE CONVERSION

Kingdom currency converts earthly assets to kingdom assets. An acre of ground can add profit to the rich man who built larger barns for himself but was "not rich toward God" (Luke 12:16–21). The same acre could be dedicated to feeding the poor in the neighborhood. What is the difference? In the second example, the acre has been converted to a kingdom asset. How? Through kingdom currency. Another example is the use of dollars to spread God's Word through written and oral Bible translation and distribution. How about the spending of earthly dollars to show God's love by sharing the gospel message with those who listen and respond by following Jesus as Savior?

I believe kingdom currency is the attitude and action of faithful stewards. It is the faithful stewardship of assets God has entrusted to you while using your resources, talents, giftedness—even your essence—while on earth. Kingdom currency is the work we do to build God's kingdom on earth and exchange earthly assets for works that last for eternity.

The steward of the acre previously mentioned determined its use. When dedicated to the purposes of God for the glory of God, the acre became a kingdom asset. If sold, neglected, or dedicated to another purpose, the same acre could just as easily revert to a mere earthly asset—of little or no kingdom value. It all depends on the faithfulness of a steward working in concert with God.

Faithful stewards use their nonphysical assets—God's Word, wisdom, love, self-control, and more—in the exercise of their stewardship currency. God has gifted each of us uniquely, adding spiritual gifts that He empowers upon salvation. These gifts and abilities from God help us steward effectively in God's kingdom.

Let me illustrate. Several years ago, Marydel and I purchased eighteen hundred acres (seven hundred fifty hectares) of land in Africa. We purchased this farm with US currency, which was exchanged into Zambian kwacha. The transaction was executed, and the seller of the land was given the kwacha. But since Marydel and I are not Zambian citizens, we could not actually own this land. We paid for it, but we did not receive the title deed. It went to our partner, John Enright, the Zambian citizen introduced in chapter 1. Together we possessed and controlled the farm, converting it to a kingdom asset.

What was the currency for this conversion? Our attitude and actions as stewards. We bought it as a base for activities we thought would further God's kingdom. Those activities included raising cattle, planting crops, and building and maintaining bee-hives for honey. This land was a tool to serve the poor of the area with employment opportunities and food.

GETTING IT FROM HERE TO HEAVEN

Finally, let's return full circle to a question raised in the middle of this chapter: How do you practically lay up your treasures in heaven? You use kingdom currency, the attitude and actions of a faithful steward. This results in doing the right things for the right reasons. These actions are prompted by—and further develop—the righteous heart that transports treasures to heaven. When God, the righteous judge, reviews your heart's attitude and your earthly actions, He will determine what burns and what endures as treasure.

Chapter 14

THE GREAT ACCOUNTING

STANDING BEFORE CHRIST

I acknowledge that God has ownership rights over all my possessions as well as over my very life. In other words, God owns me and everything I have. This awareness is a good thing, reminding me that He has provided for all my needs and that He is, and always will be, the great provider.

After having wrestled through much of my life to tear my heart away from my possessions, I now rejoice. I can see them as an honor and blessing, given to me to steward according to God's direction. And the day is coming when I will stand before Christ to give an accounting for those assets that have been entrusted to my care.

Here is a brief biblical synopsis of the accounting ahead of me—ahead of all of us.

- "From everyone who has been given much, much will be demanded" (Luke 12:48 NASB).

- "Each of us will give an account of himself to God" (Romans 14:12).
- "Each one's work will become manifest, for the Day will disclose it, because it will be revealed by fire, and the fire will test what sort of work each one has done. If the work that anyone has built on the foundation survives, he will receive a reward" (1 Corinthians 3:13–14).
- "We must all appear before the judgment seat of Christ, so that each one may receive what is due for what he has done in the body, whether good or evil" (2 Corinthians 5:10).

When I stand before the Lord to give an accounting, I don't think He is going ask, "What rate of return did you get on your investments?" Rather, He will reward me based upon my obedience to His directions. Did I steward His resources in the amounts, to whom, and when He directed? Did I remain faithful?

This future accounting has become very real to me. I think about it frequently as I self-examine to be sure I am intentional and careful in managing my portion of God's resources. I will also be required to be faithful in how I handle my assets. First Corinthians 4:2 says, "It is required of stewards that they be found faithful."

Managing God's resources requires diligent work. It's not the easy task I once suspected. Until I had enough direct experience to gain discernment, I thought giving would be easy, that stewardship was simply giving to Christian or relief organizations. But true stewardship is much more than just giving; it is entrusting assets to other faithful stewards. In the process, we are also making disciples.

Stewardship is a big job. It requires listening carefully to the Holy Spirit and acting with unflinching obedience. Once you clearly understand God's call on you to manage His resources, you realize that you have embarked on a journey, an ongoing process. It often includes stepping out in faith to let go of resources as you place them in the hands of other stewards.

Sometimes I think of myself as a stockbroker entrusted with the financial assets of a client. I can't take those assets and simply spend them on myself. Although I am entitled to a commission if I'm doing good work, the assets don't belong to me. Helping myself to them would be criminal, as many people in prison will attest. But if I invest the assets of a client to yield a return, I can anticipate three positive results: a return, a commendation, and further commissions from the client. This is what Jesus taught in the parables of the good stewards.

ACCOUNTING FOR ALL WORDS AND DEEDS

The great accounting ahead of us relates to all our words and deeds, not just our financial dealings. Our focus in this book, however, is rich men and women and our unique opportunities to manage our God-given wealth. God will judge every matter and every work, good or bad. The Old Testament book of Psalms says it this way, "You will render to a man according to his work" (62:12).

Solomon, in the book of Ecclesiastes, continued the theme. "Rejoice, O young man, in your youth, and let your heart cheer you in the days of your youth. Walk in the ways of your heart and the sight of your eyes. But know that for all these things God will bring you into judgment" (Ecclesiastes 11:9). He also wrote, "God will bring every deed into judgment, with every secret thing, whether good or evil" (12:14).

Jesus promised the same kind of accounting in Revelation 2:23: "All the churches will know that I am he who searches mind and heart, and I will give to each of you according to your works." Jesus also emphasized the complete scope and full transparency of this accounting: "Nothing is hidden that will not be made manifest, nor is anything secret that will not be known and come to light" (Luke 8:17). Jesus was signaling to all those who have eyes to see and ears to hear that an audit is coming. It will be thorough. And unavoidable. Prepare now.

Even the Nicene Creed reminds us of an accounting before the Lord Jesus Christ: "He will come again in glory to judge the living and the dead and his kingdom will have no end."[9]

If that sounds scary, it should. But the faithful steward has nothing to fear. Remember that the psalmist said that this rendering is motivated by the Lord's "steadfast love" (Psalm 62:12). The good things we've done in obedience will transfer into eternity.

Those who have built only earthly assets and not used their words and deeds for God's intended purposes will also stand before Him. I don't want to be one of them. In the intensity of God's spotlight on the uncovered truth, I imagine they will be too ashamed to attempt lame excuses. They will stand self-condemned as they see the extravagance of God's gifts to them and the magnitude of grace He offered. What they have done with their giftedness and wealth will be fully exposed. This is why the Bible so frequently repeats the warning of a future accounting: to give us an eternal perspective so we can make wise choices now.

The healthy fear I feel of standing before Jesus to account for what He has entrusted to me motivates me to be faithful. It's a fear of a loving God, who expects righteousness, justice, and accountability from me. This has been a phenomenal motivation for me to be diligent to handle all things with care, looking toward the Holy Spirit to give me guidance. It also compels me to examine His Word to find where He wants me to deploy assets into His kingdom.

---

9   "What We Believe: The Nicene Creed," The United States Conference of Catholic Bishops (website), accessed October 26, 2023, https://www.usccb.org/beliefs-and-teachings/what-we-believe.

PREPARING FOR THE FINAL EXAM

We've all taken final exams in school. There are several ways to study for them, some more effective than others. I can still hear my mom's words of wisdom: "Be sure you study all along and not wait for the last minute."

"Okay," I would say, hurrying out the door with little intention of taking it seriously. But in college, the studies got harder, the stakes grew, and I began to mature. I started studying throughout the whole semester to absorb the material and apply it as cumulative knowledge. Things made so much more sense this way. And when it came to final exam time, I was way better prepared than I had ever been cramming during panicked all-nighters.

Our stewardship can be compared to preparing for the final exam. We can give and invest during our lifetime, learning and benefiting from the wisdom of stewardship for eternity. We can use God's Word to train and discipline ourselves to be faithful givers to the work of the kingdom. My experience is that as I have exercised my ability to give, I have become a more skilled investor.

This is called the giving-while-you're-living approach. When you follow this approach, you live dangerously close to the edge of not having enough. At some point, you may even have to suspend giving large chunks because you've exhausted the pot—at least temporarily. Best partnered with anonymity and a disregard for fanfare, this approach goes beyond donorship; it is stewardship. It risks losing respect from some recipients if you're no longer able to give the large amounts you once gave. You, however, know that you gave it while you had the opportunity. High risk? Perhaps. High reward? Absolutely! Both now and in eternity. This approach has great advantages over keeping assets until we die and then turning them over for distribution through estate planning: the save-it-till-the-end approach.

The save-it-till-the-end approach is common way to distribute wealth, giving some here and there—perhaps enough to be seen as a generous donor. If you are this person, you're probably keeping most of your wealth until you die because you fear outliving your resources. Upon death, your wealth will be distributed in large chunks, earning applause from the recipients of your generosity.

Many financial experts suggest establishing a trust as a giving mechanism upon death to benefit from tax laws. But I don't think God is overly impressed with our ability to save on taxes; I think He much prefers us to give obediently all along the way. My wife has always said that it is difficult to control your estate from the grave. It also puts great pressure on our families and beneficiaries to ensure that our giving instructions are executed after our departure. The save-it-till-the-end approach feels like cramming for the final. My chosen philosophy is to invest in God's kingdom *as much and as fast as I can while I still have time*. I'd rather be well prepared and obedient when the Lord calls because this is what matters when I stand before God.

INDIVIDUAL INVESTMENTS VERSUS PORTFOLIOS

For the steward, the success of individual investments in God's kingdom is not as important as the portfolio of investments. A portfolio of investments has a long-term viewpoint and strategy. Individual investments tend to evoke more emotion based on immediate performance, much like my emotions while reading the *Wall Street Journal*.

Over a lifetime, a portfolio of investments will be much more stable and diversified, having a higher probability of positive performance. The steward investing in God's kingdom should be more attuned to the portfolio than driven by any single investment.

I have been burned with some investments in God's kingdom. They were frustrating, part of Satan's strategy to discourage me. But as soon as God's Spirit turned my eyes back to the overall portfolio, my enthusiasm was renewed by the longevity, balance, and diversification for God's kingdom.

I do not believe God's judgment of our performance will focus on individual kingdom investments—or even percentage points of return on the whole. Instead, He will look at our heart, our obedience, and a lifelong, faithful portfolio. After all, we can plant, cultivate, feed, and water, but He provides the increase.

Chapter 15

THE COMMENDATION

WHAT EVERYONE WANTS TO HEAR

"Well done, good and faithful servant!"

Every Christian wants to hear these words when standing before Jesus Christ and giving an account of their life. Most can recite these words from memory. Who wouldn't want this great commendation from Jesus? And wouldn't you hope to receive honor from those around you for having lived a righteous life while doing good for others?

Let's look at this commendation in the parable of the talents from a different perspective. Everyone wants to be complimented and commended for a job well done. The bigger question is whether we actually understand the requirements for such honors.

Many claim to be servants of the Lord. Fewer actually understand what it requires. Fewer still make it their priority to dedicate themselves to it. Servants do more than simply serve. They also yield rights and privileges. They take on a servant's heart, beginning a journey of serving at the pleasure of the

Master. There are no rights of ownership, only caretaking of the things entrusted to them.

I've sometimes heard people describe themselves as stewards. More than once I've wondered if they really earned the title. What does it embody? Is it simply managing the assets of another? I think it is nothing less than being faithful with everything you're given, including your potential and your essence. It's all of you. It is not only handling money or material possessions but also your time, giftedness, and talent in order to fulfill your purpose in God's kingdom.

Faithful stewards work diligently on earth to do what counts for eternity. It means building the kingdom by obeying what they know is true and required by God. They must abide in Christ to be able to hear the soft whispers of the Holy Spirit and develop righteous character to transport earthly treasures to heaven.

When we leave this earth, we will receive honor if we've lived to build God's kingdom. Those around us will see God's righteousness in us through our good works for the kingdom.

REGARDING RIGHTEOUSNESS

The Lord is righteous, and He loves righteous deeds. Since we do not have a righteousness of our own, God bestows upon us His own righteousness. "For our sake he made him to be sin who knew no sin, so that in him we might become the righteousness of God" (2 Corinthians 5:21).

This righteousness is a gift we receive by faith in Jesus. "The righteousness of God has been manifested apart from the law...the righteousness of God through faith in Jesus Christ for all who believe" (Romans 3:21–22).

We are made righteous through the life of Jesus because of His obedience to the Father. "Much more will those who receive the abundance of grace and the free gift of righteousness reign in life through the one man Jesus Christ" (Romans 5:17). We gain

His righteousness by abiding in Jesus Christ. We take on godly character as we walk humbly with Him. We build our godly character by obedience to the Holy Spirit's prompting and God's Word, the foundation of our righteousness.

We must realize that our righteousness is not a result of our own goodness. Even its evidence in our lives is supplied by walking in fellowship with the Holy Spirit. That's why all the wonderful qualities we work to develop are called the fruit of the Spirit: love, joy, peace, forbearance, kindness, goodness, faithfulness, gentleness, and self-control.

It's really important to understand this next sentence. Our works on earth develop our righteousness but do not provide our righteousness. Psalm 24:4–5 says, "He who has clean hands and a pure heart, who does not lift up his soul to what is false and does not swear deceitfully. He will receive blessing from the LORD and righteousness from the God of his salvation." We receive this righteousness from the God of our salvation: Jesus our Savior. Our intimate relationship with Him provides it. Then we work to match our walk with our spiritual reality, like developing a muscle.

The more we do good works with a humble spirit, the more we develop the characteristics of righteousness. "Seek first the kingdom of God and his righteousness" (Matthew 6:33). I am comforted to know that the Lord "leads me in paths of righteousness" (Psalm 23:3). He sets good works of righteousness before us as opportunities to help us develop righteous character.

Our God is a God of action. Psalm 111:2–3 says, "Great are the works of the LORD, studied by all who delight in them. Full of splendor and majesty is his work, and his righteousness endures forever." The Lord shows His righteousness through His works. He wants us to be active as well.

So our righteousness is a gift from God that we work to integrate into our daily behavior by walking in the Spirit. Jesus also pictured this as being branches in His vine. "I am the vine;

you are the branches. Whoever abides in me and I in him, he it is that bears much fruit, for apart from me you can do nothing" (John 15:5). There is no other way to develop righteousness or contribute to the kingdom.

WHAT IS THE WEALTHY PERSON TO DO?

Wealthy men and women who strive to be good stewards in God's kingdom are uniquely aware of important eternal matters. They know how to be fluid enough to respond to their opportunities to effectively deploy wealth into the kingdom. They remain unencumbered with debt or other obligations that would prohibit the timely deployment of their resources. They maintain a margin of time and are willing to commit quickly to the right opportunities. As a result, they give resources to those in need at just the right time.

Characteristics of an effective wealthy man or woman include heart attitudes of brokenness, repentance, and gratitude. Brokenness makes them responsive and useful to God. Repentance happens when they honestly examine their motives, confess their sins, and turn from them, making restitution when they can. Gratitude allows them to appreciate what God has done for them. This gratitude also extends to others, even for service easily taken for granted: like janitors in airport bathrooms, waitresses in restaurants, maids in hotels, concierges, day porters in their office buildings, and Uber drivers who take them safely to their destination.

They don't promote themselves; instead, they stand quietly and humbly before God in recognition of His greatness. These effective wealthy men and women of God's kingdom must hear from their Master. They diligently search for their next assignment in His kingdom, searching and applying the Scriptures as they listen to the whispers of the Holy Spirit to discern what God intends them to do.

The rich of this world are to be stewards for the future. "As for the rich in this present age, charge them not to be haughty, nor to set their hopes on the uncertainty of riches, but on God, who richly provides us with everything to enjoy. They are to do good, to be rich in good works, to be generous and ready to share, thus storing up treasure for themselves as a good foundation for the future, so that they may take hold of that which is truly life" (1 Timothy 6:17–19). This advice will help us manage wealth for maximum value now and maximum reward forever.

EFFECTIVE KINGDOM STEWARDS

Effective kingdom stewards work diligently, as exhorted by Paul, "Work out your own salvation with fear and trembling" (Philippians 2:12). Known for their consistent, dependable effort, they do not sit in lazy complacency.

Effective stewards look for ways to work with other stewards. There is companionship, comradery, and community when they find other like-minded men and women. They joyfully join others to accomplish the purposes God sets before them. While on their own journey of stewardship, they are like magnets attracting others to do good work. Avoiding jealousy, they recognize what is their portion to steward as well as where they can partner with others. They are always on the lookout for fields with buried treasure; when they find one, they share it with other stewards to maximize its benefit.

Stewards also know to heed Jesus' words in Matthew 7:6: "Do not give dogs what is holy, and do not throw your pearls before pigs, lest they trample them underfoot and turn to attack you." Sometimes handling treasures requires shrewdness. Wise stewards don't simply give in to those who destroy, misuse, or waste; they entrust these treasures to others who will use them wisely.

God uses well-equipped, prepared, excellent men and women for His kingdom work. It is good to work hard, to strive for excellence in everything, and to continually prepare for future kingdom work. Stewards should neither denounce themselves in false humility nor be arrogant or prideful of accomplishments. Instead, "be honest in your estimate of yourselves, measuring your value by how much faith God has given you" (Romans 12:3 TLB). Humility is always the best attribute for working in God's kingdom. Remember that no matter how greatly you are gifted, the attribute is still a gift rather than something self-created.

The lifestyle of stewards is characterized by the second part of the Great Commandment: loving their neighbors as themselves. This combats selfishness, enabling us to fulfill New Testament commands like this one: "Do not neglect to do good and to share what you have, for such sacrifices are pleasing to God" (Hebrews 13:16).

Stewards aspire to live quietly, witnessing to others through their productive work as they exemplify godly principles. Because they trust God to meet their needs, they are not reluctant to share what He provides.

Stewards recognize that righteousness and justice are the foundation of God's throne. Our efforts to righteously pursue justice—especially on behalf of the vulnerable—are more acceptable to the Lord than any sacrifices we make. We are to maintain the rights of the afflicted and destitute while rescuing the weak and delivering them from the hand of the wicked. God's kingdom becomes evident through the righteousness and justice of stewards, enabling the culture around them to flourish.

Life is hard. This truth is an inescapable reality in our fallen world. But through our struggles and toil we develop the character God has uniquely designed for each of us. As we develop it in keeping with His Word, we gain a heart of righteousness that transports treasures to heaven.

THE RACE

My personal running experiences have taught me about preparing for heaven. Excitement builds prior to any race as the anticipation ramps up, forcing adrenaline through the system. This seems to peak with the sound of the starting horn, especially in longer races, giving way to a sense of relief as the running actually starts. I love the length of half-marathons, which in my better days would take about two hours. Now, I have to add an extra thirty minutes.

At some point in the middle, I feel like I'm going to die. Fatigue almost always lurks at mile nine. And then there are the dreaded hills. Almost indiscernible in a car, they feel like mountains when I'm running up them, and the race never seems to include the descent. And they appear at the most inopportune times, when I'm already spent. But I know from experience that the finish line is coming. And so is relief from the pain—eventually. Even better, I'll enjoy the satisfaction of knowing I ran to the best of my ability and that there is a shiny medal waiting.

In our long race toward heaven, some hills seem to be more than we can bear. The pain is greater than we expected, and it feels as though it will be permanent. And the reward? It's kind of hard to get our heads around that. Whatever He is preparing for us in the future will be mind-boggling.

So, if we want to hear these famous words when we stand before Christ to give an accounting, we must embark on a lifelong, faithful journey of managing everything for an eternal impact in His kingdom. Anything less falls short of being the good and faithful servant.

WHAT'S AT THE FINISH LINE?

Consider these words from the apostle Paul, near the end of his life, to Timothy, his disciple and mentee: "I have fought the good fight, I have finished the race, I have kept the faith. Henceforth there is laid up for me the crown of righteousness, which the Lord, the righteous judge, will award to me on that day" (2 Timothy 4:7–8). Paul was telling Timothy that he endured until the end, that he was a conqueror of the things of the flesh and of this world so that he might receive the prize in the future. Paul went on to say that the same promise applies to all who live with eternity, the Lord's return, in mind.

The reward for the faithful is not only a commendation but also the crown of righteousness. Those who receive this crown of righteousness will cast it at the feet of Jesus in gratitude as they honor Him in His infinite glory.

Just imagine looking into the eyes of Jesus, who welcomes you to live with Him surrounded by "pleasures forevermore" (Psalm 16:11). You watch as others cast their crowns of righteousness at His feet in unbridled joy and gratitude. The crown of righteousness is not just some kind of merit badge to show off our accomplishments. It is the sincerest expression possible of love and gratitude. It says, "You changed my life forever, and I have done my best to live for you. Even the righteousness signified by this crown is a gift from you."

A BENEDICTION

Let these beautiful words from "When I Survey the Wondrous Cross" by Isaac Watts begin our benediction.

> My richest gain I count but loss
> and pour contempt on all my pride.
> Forbid it, Lord, that I should boast…
> Love so amazing, so divine,
> demands my soul, my life, my all.

It is my prayer that this book has encouraged you. I pray the words of Moses from Psalm 90:17, "Yes, establish the work of our hands!" This liturgical prayer says it well: "Through Christ and with all your saints, we offer ourselves and our lives to your service. Send us out in the power of your Spirit, to stand with you in your world."[10]

May God drive deeply into the hearts of faithful men and women the desire to emerge as conduits of His goodness in doing His work. May faithful men and women put their hands to the plow, assisting other faithful workers to accomplish God's work within His economy.

May God equip you with "every good thing" so that you will be pleasing in His sight, one day entering His presence to cast your crown of righteousness before the Lord Jesus Christ while hearing multitudes sing "Holy, Holy, Holy! Lord God Almighty" by Reginald Heber and "Crown Him with Many Crowns" by Matthew Bridges and Godfrey Thring:

> Holy, holy, holy! All the saints adore Thee,
> casting down their golden crowns around the glassy sea;
> cherubim and seraphim falling down before Thee,
> which wert and art and evermore shall be.
>
> Crown Him with many crowns,
> the Lamb upon His throne.
> Hark! How the heavenly anthem drowns
> all music but its own.
> Awake, my soul, and sing
> of him who died for thee,
> and hail Him as thy matchless king
> through all eternity.

As you watch the multitudes sing, you know this is just the beginning for you in God's eternal kingdom. It's not that you've

10   *Sunday Service Bulletin* (Jackson Hole, WY: St. John's Episcopal Church), September 8, 2019, https://www.stjohnsjackson.org/uploads/files/sept-8-2019-10am_284.pdf, 8.

lived a good life and gone to heaven where your movie end credits roll, but you are now a supporting actor in God's great movie forevermore.

ACKNOWLEDGMENTS

I would like to dedicate this book to the men of my Wednesday afternoon Bible study: Mark, Tom, Mike, Bob, Holt, Nick, Daryl, Ross, Jim, and Ted.

I am inadequate without Marydel, a precious soul, my partner in God's kingdom, and the sharpener of my character.

This book would not have been possible without my faithful assistant, Lisa Vasquez, and the skillful editing of Steve D. Gardner.

ABOUT THE AUTHOR

Raymond H. Harris is an architect, executive movie and music producer, and venture capitalist in God's kingdom. He is founder of one of the largest architectural firms specializing in corporate architecture. The firm was ranked as the number two retail design firm in America for three years.

As one of the most prolific American architects, Raymond uses his profit to build economic engines and ignite young men and women to develop influential businesses in entertainment, agriculture, manufacturing, and technology. He is deploying assets to build God's kingdom on earth as much and as fast as he can.

Raymond is a Senior Fellow of the Institute for Global Engagement at Dallas Baptist University. He graduated first in his class from the University of Oklahoma and was selected as the outstanding senior and distinguished alumnus in the College of Architecture. Raymond serves on numerous corporate and nonprofit boards and is extensively involved in sustainable community development projects in Africa and Asia.

Raymond is the author of *The Heart of Business* and *Business by Design*. He is also an executive producer for numerous movies distributed by Sony Pictures and Lionsgate. Raymond has hiked all the national parks in the continental US, has served as a Boy Scout scoutmaster, and has run over fifty half-marathons.

Raymond and his wife, Marydel, have four adult children, who are married, and ten grandchildren. They reside in Dallas, Texas, and Jackson Hole, Wyoming.